Little Red Book
of
Perfect Written English

By the same author

Little Red Book Series

Little Red Book of Slang-Chat Room Slang

Little Red Book of English Vocabulary Today

Little Red Book of Grammar Made Easy

Little Red Book of English Proverbs

Little Red Book of Prepositions

Little Red Book of Idioms and Phrases

Little Red Book of Euphemisms

Little Red Book of Effective Speaking Skills

Little Red Book of Modern Writing skills

Little Red Book of Verbal Phrases

Little Red Book of Synonyms

Little Red Book of Antonyms

Little Red Book of Common Errors

Little Red Book of Punctuation

Little Red Book of Letter Writing

Little Red Book of Essay Writing

A2Z Book Series

A2Z Quiz Book

A2Z Book of Word Origins

Others

The Book of Fun Facts

The Book of More Fun Facts

The Book of Firsts and Lasts

The Book of Virtues

The Book of Motivation

Read Write Right: Common Errors in English

The Students' Companion

Little Red Book *of* Perfect Written English

Terry O'Brien

RUPA

Published by
Rupa Publications India Pvt. Ltd 2012
7/16, Ansari Road, Daryaganj
New Delhi 110002

Sales centres:
Allahabad Bengaluru Chennai
Hyderabad Jaipur Kathmandu
Kolkata Mumbai

Copyright © Terry O'Brien 2012

All rights reserved.
No part of this publication may be reproduced, transmitted,
or stored in a retrieval system, in any form or by any means, electronic,
mechanical, photocopying, recording or otherwise,
without the prior permission of the publisher.

ISBN: 978-81-291-2054-0

Second impression 2015

10 9 8 7 6 5 4 3 2

The moral right of the author has been asserted.

Printed at Shree Maitrey Printech Pvt. Ltd., Noida

This book is sold subject to the condition that it shall not, by way of trade
or otherwise, be lent, resold, hired out, or otherwise circulated, without the
publisher's prior consent, in any form of binding or cover other than that in
which it is published.

*I dedicate this book to late Prof. A.P. O'Brien,
my father, friend, guide and mentor, who
inspired me to the canon of excellence:
re-imagining what's essential*

PREFACE

PERFECT WRITTEN ENGLISH is a book to improve your writing style. Everything can be said. But how about saying it clearly! This is a handbook that tells all you need to write fluently and convincingly: the correct way to the most clear and persuasive structure for an argument. Do put your message across elegantly and effectively!

Remember — Perfection isn't attainable — just do the best you can.

'Grasp beyond your reach, or what's a heaven for!'

Word File
(Parts of Speech)

I. WORDS
(also called 'parts of speech')

The BIG FOUR

Nouns

Nouns are things, places or concepts. Dog, Mumbai, patience. Nouns can be singular (a dog) or plural (two or more dogs).

Verbs

Verbs are actions or descriptions of states. Verbs are grammatically the most complex words; they come in many forms: 'tenses', 'voices 'moods'.

Adjectives

Adjectives tell us something about or 'qualify' nouns (green forest, blue sky, sad look).

Adverbs

Adverbs tell us something about verbs (ran quickly, coming soon) or adjectives (He was grossly fat).

Word Roles

A simple word like *round* can play the role of a noun, verb, adjective, adverb or, a preposition.

You bought the drinks last time; now it's my *round.(noun)*
The tiger suddenly *rounded* on its trainer. *(verb)*
The world is *round*. *(adjective)*
He looked *round,* but still couldn't see if he was being followed. *(adverb)*
The host showed me *round* the house herself. *(preposition)*

After the BIG FOUR it gets a bit more complex.

Pronouns 'stand in' for nouns in various ways.

- *Personal pronouns*: I, you, he, she etc., but also *me* and *mine*.
- *Demonstrative pronouns*, so called because they are often used when showing something, as in: **This** is my book.
- *Interrogative pronouns,* which ask questions: **Where** am I?
- *Relative pronouns,* which relate groups of words to nouns: **Who:** The person who did that.
- There are also *'indefinite' pronouns*—words like *nobody, either*.

Note, again, that a word can 'be' more than one kind of pronoun:

- **That** is a demonstrative pronoun in *That's* mine!
- Also a relative pronoun in *The idea that I had yesterday.*

Two terms:

- The noun for which a pronoun is standing in is called *antecedent*.
- The *standing-in process*: She is my cousin, the pronoun *she* is said to 'refer to' Irene.

> **Conjunctions** *link words*, usually of similar types, for example two nouns (bread and butter) or two adjectives: Since you were going to Dubai, and I had to leave for Muscat at the same time, we shared the taxi.

You can begin a sentence with a conjunction. *And finally, I'd like to thank Mr Mehra...* is simply linking a new sentence to something that has gone before.

> **Prepositions** *link* words, as conjunctions do. They often say something about *how, why, when* or *where* something happened.

For example:
 The car was removed by the cops. (how)
 The car was removed by mistake. (why)
 I want that car removed by three o'clock... (when)
 .....and left by the garage, where it belongs. (where)

Prepositions often *link nouns to other parts of the sentence* (by the cops, by the garage etc.).

> ***Determiners*** come in front of nouns. Examples of determiners are what used to be called 'quantifiers': some books, no problem, every time, all people that live in China—and the **definite and indefinite articles,** *the* and *a.*

The two articles, *the* and *a*, have a silent power. **A** car means one of all the cars out there; which one is not specified (hence the name indefinite article). **The** car implies we are talking about a specific, definite vehicle. This focuses our attention more—we're talking about a particular one.

A car went past the window. We haven't heard of this car before. We don't know anything else about it, and may not hear of it again.

Groups of Words

If the word is the basic unit of sense in a piece of writing, the next level up is the sentence.

A Sentence

☞ begins with a capital letter
☞ ends with a proper mark
☞ contains a verb.

A sentence has to include a **finite verb.** A finite verb is a verb that has a subject. *But don't lose too much sleep over this examination. I never have.*

Other Terms for Groups of Words:

> A group of words **without a finite verb** is a **phrase.** The yellow Jeep came slowly down the slope is a sentence. In that sentence, *the yellow Jeep* is a phrase, and so is *slowly down the slope*.

Phrases can do the jobs of nouns (Loving you is easy), of adverbs (The food packets arrived right on time), or of adjectives (Thrilled with joy, he leapt into the Ganges).

A **fragment** is a phrase dressed up as a sentence—in other words beginning with a capital and ending with a full stop, but lacking a finite verb.

A clause is a group of words that contains a finite verb but is not a full-fledged sentence (it has no capital at the start or no full stop at the end). There are **two types of clause**s: *main* and *subordinate*. **Main clauses** make sense by their selves; **subordinates clauses** don't. In the sentence: *The dog sat on the carpet which I cleaned yesterday,* the words *the dog sat on the carpet* are the **main clause,** while *which I cleaned yesterday* is a **subordinate clause**.

The words *at* is the verb in the main clause, is called the **main verb** while *cleaned* is called a *dependent verb*.

If a sentence is formed by joining two main clauses (The dog sat on the carpet and left off a lot of ticks), there are two main verbs.

Subordinate clauses, like phrases, can do the work of parts of speech. They can act as *nouns* (What I like about you is your honesty), as *adverbs* (He opened the letter when I gave it to him) or as *adjectives* (He finally met Allen, who had become his sister's best friend at school). This last type of subordinate clause, telling us something more about a noun, is also called *relative clause*.

Taking sentences to bits......PARSING

> The classic formula: SVO: Subject, Verb, Object. The lion ate the deer, *The* is the subject, *ate* is the verb and the unfortunate *deer* is the object.

Two types of **object—direct; indirect**.

In the sentence: She gave the book to Nikita, the book is the *direct object* (The thing that she gave is the direct object and Nikita is the indirect object (the person to whom the book was given).

Parsing is called a **complement.** These are words that follow verbs that are about 'states' rather than actions: State verb: *I am a writer*, *I* is clearly the subject and *am* is clearly the verb, but it feels a little odd to call a writer object. 'Object' implies being on the receiving end of something, rather than just being a state. So we call *a writer* in this sentence the complement.

Note that complements can also be adjectives. *I am hungry*—subject, verb, complement. Other examples of 'state' verbs followed by complements might be *I feel unwell*; *the weather remains bad!*

Distinction between **simple** and **complex sentences:** **Simple sentences** are basically just main clauses. I went out for the evening. **Complex sentences** are a main clause plus one or more subordinate clauses and/or one or more main clauses joined to it.

Examples:

Two main clauses: He took out his car and went out for a long drive.

Main plus subordinate: He took out his car, which made the garage door slam open.

Two mains plus subordinate: He slammed the garage door, which made the drum fall off the corner and went out into the rain.

Three little words we often see,
Determiners, like a, an and the.

A **Noun's** the name of anything,
A school or garden, hoop or string.

An **Adjective** tells the kind of noun,
Like great, small, pretty, white or brown.

Instead of nouns the **Pronouns** stand—
John's head, his face, my arm, your hand.

Verbs tell of something being done,
To read, write, count, sing, jump or run.

How things are done, the **Adverbs** tell,
Like slowly, quickly, ill or well.

A **Preposition** stands before
A noun, as in a room, or through a door.

Conjunctions join the nouns together,
Like boy or girl, wind and weather.

The **Interjection** shows surprise,
Like Oh! How charming. Ah! How wise!

The whole are called **'Nine Parts of Speech'**,
Which reading, writing and speaking teach.

II. Punctuation

'The Zero Tolerance Approach': There are rules, and they need to be followed.

Punctuation is a tool to make writing clearer.

'Big Four'

There are four main punctuation marks:
- comma
- semicolon
- colon
- full stop

These are 'units of pause':
- **A comma** is one unit
- a **semicolon** two units
- a **colon** three units
- a **full stop** is four.

NOTE: A semicolon is two units and a colon two-and-a-half, jumping to four for the full stop.

The **COMMA** is the basic unit of pause. Its main use is to divide complex sentence into its basic parts.

- I will discuss tomorrow, if that is okay with you.
- By cutting down expenses such as advertisement or promotion types of training, one can make the profits of a company look much healthier than it actually is.

> *NOTE:*
> ☞ In the first example, the comma is grammatically necessary;it separates two clauses, one main and one subordinate.
> ☞ In the second the correct point pause in a long, and rather weighty sentence.

Commas are also used for bracketing off *non-essential parts of sentence*.
- Mr Ahmed, who seemed to be in a great hurry, ran past without saying hello.
- The stolen money, however, was never found.

A comma is needed when a sentence is *turned round so that subordinate clause* is put before a main clause.
- Before turning on the main road driver, please read the instructions.

The comma can be used for *emphasis:*
- Rita came into the room, slowly.

Take the comma away, and what matters is that Rita came in, how she did it, which is a kind of afterthought!

Commas shouldn't separate subjects and verbs

Rita, came into the room slowly.

> *NOTE:* Punctuation is a Guiding Principle.

> The **semicolon** is the most underused punctuation mark around.

It is generally used for joining two main clauses with different subjects:
- *I went to the village; you were on the same bus too.*
- *Reading is good; writing is better*

> The **colon** is a slightly bigger divider than the semi. It's used:

☞ To introduce lists:
☞ When a sentence builds up to a piece of information:
  • There's only one way she ever entered rooms: slowly.
☞ The colon is also used to introduce a formal quote.
  • As Shakespeare said: 'All the world's a stage...'

> The **full stop** is less complex: End of sentence. **The Americans call it, a 'period'.**

The full stop also has some **odd uses**: in abbreviations like (= et cetera) and i.e.

Others

> **Apostrophes** Their correct use is for possessives (Rita's desk) and where words have been contracted (don't).

☞ It's and its.
  • The dog ate its dinner. (possessive)
  • It's raining! (contraction of it is)
☞ **Plurals of acronyms**. An acronym is a 'word' made out of an abbreviation of two or more pre-existing words, such as CD-compact disc. Its plural is CDs, not CD's.

> **Question marks** are needed in direct speech but not in indirect (reported) speech.

  • He asked, 'Which route is for Agra?'
          But
  • He asked which route was for Agra.

Exclamation marks are easy to overdo, especially when you trying to sound informal. They get used a lot in **emails**.)

The **dash** is informal, more like conversation.

The **hyphen** is used to make new words by joining existing ones. Examples: user-friendly, fast-moving, extra-special etc.

The **three dots at the end** of a sentence/paragraph are called an **ellipsis**. The sense is of something more to be said, but left out because the reader either knows it already, or can guess.

Inverted commas are used for speech, and also as a gentle way of bracketing words.

- "Right," said Rosy.
- Rosy said, "Right."

Single inverted commas is used for **softer bracketing.**

Single inverted commas are also used when the writer is being **sarcastic**:
- The Government's false 'white paper' was indeed useless.

Italics are used to highlight something. Underlining is a bit loud. Titles of books or films are often written in italics.

III. Grammatical Errors

'Grammar' is basically the rules that make language work.

Verbs not Agreeing with Subjects

The rule is simple: the verb 'agrees with' the subject.
- Singular subject, singular verb: The dog *sits* on the carpet.
- Plural subject, plural verb: The dogs *sit* on the carpet.
- Two singular subjects, plural verb: The cat and the dog *sit* on the carpet.

NOTE: There are **'irregular' verbs** like sit on the carpet (I am sitting on the carpet, you are sitting etc.).

- **'Collective' nouns**, take singular nouns that mean a group of individual beings or items.
  (A) The team <u>is</u> working on it or
  (B) The team <u>are</u> working on it?

NOTE: Technically A is right, but B has become acceptable, as what is really being said is (The people in) the team are working on it.

Company names have a similar problem. Technically, they are singular.
- Microsoft is one of the largest companies in the world.
  But
- Microsoft are trying to get involved in every aspect of computing. *Generally, people stick to the singular.*

> *NOTE:* Sometimes, when the massiveness of the company is being highlighted, writers drift into the plural:

Double subjects can cause difficulties.
- Kapish and I *are* going shopping is easy: there are two of us, so the verb is plural.

> *NOTE:* Some people even mess that up by saying *Kapish* and *me* are going shopping.

> *NOTE:* But what if it's just one of us, Kapish or I...? Kapish or I am going shopping sounds odd but is actually technically correct, because the rule is that the verb agrees with the nearer subject.

We may try to rephrase saying something like
- Either Kapish is going shopping or I am.

> *NOTE:* When subjects and complements are different numbers, the basic 'agreement' rule remains: the verb agrees with the subject.

- Computer games *are* his only interest.
- His only interest *is* computer games.

None, either, neither (and all other 'indefinite pronouns') are singular.
- None of us *has* the answer.
- Neither of us *has* the answer.

Unbalanced Sentences

If using 'correlative conjunctions'—which is the technical term for constructions like either. . . or.. . or not only... but also...make sure each 'arm' of the expression bears the same weight that works correctly with the rest of the sentence.

For example:
☞ We require students of either French or native speakers.

should be

- We require either students of French or native speakers.

'Who' or 'whom'?

Whom is technically the correct word:
- To whom am I speaking?

To get technical for a moment, you use **whom** if it refers to object (direct or indirect) of the relative clause. So:
☞ The man whom I mentioned yesterday. (The man is the *direct object* of mentioned, the verb in the relative clause.)
- The man about whom I talked yesterday. (The man is the indirect object of the verb in the relative clause: I talked about him.)

Remember that **whom** is only used where it refers to the one of the relative clause, so the man who sold me the car (the man is subject of the relative clause: he sold the car to me) is, of course both correct and natural-sounding.

'That' or 'which'?

- The lorry that drove past the house yesterday was green. The lorry which drove past the house yesterday was green.

NOTE: Answering the first question, the first sentence is correct; the second sentence will be correct when two commas have been inserted, so that it reads:

- The lorry, which drove past the house yesterday, was green.

The two sentences have subtly different meanings.

If one said *The lorry that drove past the house yesterday was green,* people would know nothing about this lorry at the start of the sentence, but by the end would have learned two things—that it drove past the house yesterday, and that it was green.

If one said *The lorry, which drove past the house yesterday, was green,* people would be right to ask, 'What lorry?' The force of the 'which' and the commas is to tell the listeners that they should already know something about this lorry, and they are now being told some extra things.

IV. Spelling

Most people now work on computers with **spellcheckers.** It makes life easier—you no longer have to remember how many *m's* there are in 'accommodation'—but it also makes spelling even less pardonable. *'Whoever wrote the mis-spelt document that has just landed on my desk couldn't even be bothered to use a simple computer function!'* However:

Don't forget that some mis-spellings slip past the spell checker you type in:
- *I was so glad to receive a letter **form** you* (spot the mistake) (FORM/FROM)

The spellchecker just sees ten recognisable words and moves; the grammar checker, those green wavy lines tells us that our sentences are too long, doesn't seem to find a problem with this either.

☞ <u>Spellcheckers can object to perfectly correct use.</u> For example, it didn't like mis-spelt above, objecting to mis. But that's a perfectly acceptable way of writing the word.

☞ <u>Make sure your spellchecker is set to US or UK English,</u> depending on your readership.

There are some areas that your spellchecker will not help you with...

—ise and—ize

Should you write *organize* or *organise*? *Advertize* or *advertise*? *Magnetize* or *magnetize*?

The answer is that it depends. Some verbs absolutely require—*ise*. Others should technically be—*ize* but can be either.

And there are some in the middle. But the rules are not all clear—verbs have to end in—ise.

- First, of course, verbs like *practice* that don't end in the *'ize'* sound. But there are others—*advertise, advise, apprise, chastise, circumcise, comprise, compromise, despise, devise, enfranchise, excise, exercise, improvise, revise, supervise, surmise and surprise*. From the other end,—*ize* is correct when existing nouns or adjectives have been converted into verbs by adding a suffix (the Ancient Greeks started it, with the suffix—*izein*) with the sense of 'to make something.'

> *NOTE:* Other words, like organize/organise: In America,—ize is preferred. In the UK, the trend is towards using—ise. *Organize* is actually original form (mediaeval Latin, *organizare*!)

Licence, license, practise, practice

C is the noun, **s** the verb.

- Sadly it was not the man's practice to practise what he preached.
- 'Licensed premises' have been granted a licence to sell alcohol.

Enquiry, inquiry

An *inquiry* is a formal procedure; an *enquiry* is simply a question verb—to enquire. Better—but to use the word *ask*!

Effect, affect

The **noun** is now always *effect* (though there was once a noun affect, which meant an emotion). The **verb** is usually to *affect*.

> *NOTE:* To affect means either 'to put something on for show':

- He affected an American accent

or 'to have an effect on'.

- Rain affected his moodswings.

There's also a not hugely common verb to effect, meaning 'to bring something about':

- They effected an amazing turn around in their business.

Principal, principle

Principal is an adjective meaning 'most important'; a *principle* is a moral belief.

- A principal is the head of an institution.
- The college principal's principle was that of justice.

Stationary, stationery

Stationary is the *adjective* (standing still); stationery the *noun* (pens, paper etc.).

Dependant, dependent

Note here, the 'a' is the noun and the 'e' is the adjective.

- Jacob's dependants were dependent on him.

Counsel, council

Counsel is *advice* (and the *verb* to counsel, to advise)

- Councils are legislative bodies, peopled by counsellors.

Complement, compliment

A complement is <u>a full amount</u> as in:
- The regiment set off for battle with its complement of men.

As a <u>verb, complement usually means 'goes well with'</u>:
- His teacher complemented his striped blazer and tie.
- Compliments are nice things people say.

Ordinance, ordnance

An <u>ordinance is a command; ordnance means military material, guns</u>:

Aural, oral

<u>Aural is to do with ears</u>; <u>oral with mouths</u>.

Confused words

The pairs of words that mean different but sound the same are **homophones:**
<u>formerly and formally, idol and idle, potable, portable, presence and presents, wails and whales.</u>

A related topic is that of words that sound almost the same but not quite, and which get confused and/or misused. Words like:

Enormousness and enormity

Enormousness just means 'bigness'.
- *So why do intelligent people who should know better talk about the enormity of the task in preparing for competitive examinations?*

Mitigate and militate

Mitigating circumstances are <u>those which lessen the responsibility</u> someone has for a crime (or in some sense make it more understandable). To _militate_ is to have an effect, as in:

* *The recent scams have not militated against the Prime Minister's popularity.*

Imply and infer

To imply is to make a hint; to infer is to take a hint.

Prescribe, proscribe

* Your doctor prescribes medicine, but proscribes (prohibits) smoking and drinking.

Continuous, continual

Continuous means unending; continual means very frequent.

Flaunt and flout

To flaunt something is to show it off, in a crude and excessive way.

* Peacocks flaunt their tails.

To flout is to ignore a rule, deliberately and slightly provocatively—

* The teenager flouted the no-smoking signs and lit a cigarette.

V. Style

How to write English that is not just free of mistakes (the right place to start).

<u>Good writing is all about getting your readers into this state, and keeping them there.</u>

- ♦ The Golden Rule to achieve this is: Every word should lead your reader forward.

The Golden Rule

☞ Every: This sets up certain expectations in the reader: some kind of Generalisation follows. Every what?

☞ Word. Now we know. Actually, I would like to say more than the 'word'.

☞ Every punctuation mark should be leading your reader forward, too.

☞ Should. Obviously this shows that one is laying down the law. 'Should' implies an obligation, but not such an iron one 'must':
- ♦ Perfection isn't attainable; just do the best you can.

☞ Lead: The main verb in a sentence has often the most power: so choose a verb that is as clear and specific as possible. Good writing is leadership.

☞ Your: To say *your* read makes the additional point that readers have a relationship with you.

☞ Reader: The object of the sentence, another key word.

☞ Forward: You will lead your readers forward, towards goals you clearly understand.

Before you start a piece, you must have a clear idea of what you want your readers to know; and when you call a piece 'finished', you must have a strong conviction that the piece conveys this knowledge.

The three most common and damaging flow-stoppers: ambiguity, repetition and jargon.

Ambiguity

At best, ambiguity is comical:
- We're delighted to announce the appointment of Nikita.

The reader is puzzled!

The most powerful tool for battling ambiguity is the ability to the stand back from what you have just written and try to see it from the reader's viewpoint. The magic question is 'Does this say what I want it to?'

A major cause of ambiguity is <u>wandering pronouns</u>:

Nikita came into the room and sat next to Rosy. She was very unhappy.

Who was unhappy? Probably Nikita, as she is the subject of the first sentence, but some readers might see Rosy right next to the *her*, and draw the opposite conclusion. Re-phrase this.

Here are Nikita and Rosy again:
- Rosy sat in the old chair. Nikita came in and sat next to her. She was very unhappy.

Repetition

<u>Unnecessary repetition breaks the</u> Golden Rule that every word should lead your reader forward. Unnecessary

repetition doesn't lead the reader anywhere—except towards boredom.

1. Re-phrase (usually the best way).
2. Simply leave out unnecessary repetitions.
3. Use pronouns—when you can do so with zero ambiguity.
4. Use a few synonyms.
5. Use 'the former' and 'the latter'.

Example:
- *There are differences between mainland Chinese and overseas Chinese. The mainland Chinese tend to think of all Chinese including the overseas Chinese as part of the Chinese cultural family. The overseas Chinese are more aware of the political differences between mainland China and the countries of the Chinese diaspora, though they are aware that they share an underlying common cultural heritage with the mainland Chinese.*

Rewriting this, we get:
- There are differences between mainland and overseas Chinese (simple rephrasing). The mainlanders (another simple re-phrase: we have established that we are talking about Chinese) tend to think of all Chinese (fine to restate 'Chinese' here—don't be too afraid of repetition and wander off into flights of fancy like 'sons and daughters of the Middle Kingdom'), wherever they are in the world, (another re-phrase) as part of one (it's obviously Chinese) cultural family. Overseas Chinese (again, fine to restate 'Chinese', especially as 'overseas Chinese' is pretty much a stock phrase) are more aware of the political contrasts

(synonym, avoiding repetition of 'differences') between mainland China and the countries of the diaspora (obviously, from the context, the Chinese diaspora), though, they are aware that they share an underlying (have left out 'common cultural', as that is another unnecessary repetition: if they share it, it is 'common'; and heritage.

Or, without the comments:
- There are differences between mainland and overseas Chinese. The mainlanders tend to think of all Chinese, wherever they are in the world, as part of one cultural family. Overseas Chinese are more aware of the political contrasts between mainland China and the countries of the diaspora, though they are aware that they share an underlying heritage.

Re-writing is not always just a one-step process.
- There are differences between mainland and overseas Chinese. The mainlanders tend to think of all Chinese, wherever they are in the world, as part of one cultural family. Overseas Chinese are more aware of the political contrasts between mainland China and the countries of the diaspora.

Jargon

There are **two sorts of jargon:** Both impolite and destructive!

One type is the **inappropriate use of technical terms.** There is nothing wrong with using technical terms when communicating exclusively with fellow technicians. Here are a few lines from a report on a cricket match:

Tendulkar lofted the bowler over mid-on twice in the over. He next found himself facing the bowler. He pushed the ball forward to a googly with uncharacteristic tentativeness and lobbed a bat-pad chance to silly-mid-off with ease.

Use the following techniques:
- ☞ Flag up that it's a technical term, so the reader doesn't feel stupid.
- ☞ Explain the term the first time you introduce it.
- ☞ Use diagrams or pictures. If it's computer-related, show what the user's screen will look like.
- ☞ Have a glossary at the end.
- ☞ Have an index.

OVER BURDENED JARGON

- alleviate
- documentation
- increment
- on-going
- utilise
- avail oneself of
- with respect to
- concerning
- due to the fact that
- necessitate
- indebtedness
- currently
- augment
- initiate

Clear English

- lessen
- documents, papers
- pay rise
- continuing
- use
- if it happens
- use
- about
- because
- require
- debt
- buy
- now
- increase
- begin

Making Your Writing Lively

12 ways to make your writing lively: Lively writing engages and pleases the reader.

Use the Active Voice

- In 'Kapish hit Ravi' the verb is in the active voice.
- In 'Ravi was hit by Kapish' the verb is in the passive voice

<u>Lively writing uses the active voice.</u> Of any scene, we ask three basic questions:
- ☞ <u>Who's</u> doing the action?
- ☞ <u>What</u> are they doing?
- ☞ <u>To whom?</u> (Or to what?)

The **passive voice** is used all the time in <u>business and official writing</u>.
- It has been decided to refuse your application...
- A recommendation has been made by the inspectors that...

There's something oddly dispiriting about the passive voice.

There are circumstances when the passive voice is useful.

☞ <u>First,</u> when someone has been the victim of circumstances and you wish to show the fact:
- Walking home from the park, he was knocked down by a drunk driver.

☞ <u>Second,</u> the passive can help make paragraphs cohere.

☞ <u>Third,</u> passives can get you out of the 'dangling participle' problem:
- ✗ Cycling along a path used by Jim Corbett, a leopard leapt out and attacked me.

A passive will stop this sounding silly:
- ✓ Cycling along a path used by Jim Corbett, I was attacked by a leopard.

☞ <u>Fourth,</u> you may genuinely not know the 'subject' of an action.

☞ And <u>finally,</u> yes, you may want to hide behind a passive voice. If this is the case, at least do so knowingly.

Use positive not negative verbs:
- ✗ The teacher says to the class: Close your eyes.

Avoid

- ✓ Don't think of a purple cow! Don't!

To get the negative, one has to go via the positive: But why take this long route? Our natural information-processing technique is to look for subject/verb/object and create some picture model of it:
- Toilets are not to be used, except for customers.

Negatives get worse once they start stacking up. Double negatives can be hell to unscramble.
- ✗ It is unusual for us not to do well in such circumstances.

Double negatives can also be ambiguous.
- Do not use this extinguisher in cases of electrical malfunction

but

provide users with a positive alternative as well:
— use the green one instead.

Be as specific as you can

- The woman got out of the car, put her bag over her shoulder and walked across the road-tells you very little.

Keep Learning New Words

Keep on building your working knowledge of the English language.

Here are <u>three questions to ask when getting to know a new word:</u>
1. What are its implications, its echoes?
2. Is it only used in certain contexts?
3. How well known is it?

Use simile, metaphor and analogy

A simile is a poetic, imaginative comparison: My love is like a red, red rose.

A metaphor is a more condensed version of this, where a comparison has been turned into a word in the main phrase:

- The soldier is a lion.

An ***analogy*** is when one understood concept or process is used to explain another, mysterious concept or process by pointing out similarities.

Similes and metaphors are more tools for the artistic writer—the novelist, the poet, the dramatist—than the non-fiction writer.

'Mixed metaphors', and unintentionally <u>comic lines</u> such as:

- The government has tried to grab the bull by the horns but has ended up with egg on its face.

Be assertive

If you've got something to say, say it! Cut out those phrases *I should like to, we will try to, we wish to inform you:*

<u>We wish to inform you</u> that your January payment is overdue.

No.

- Your January payment is overdue

Prune

Pruning is a great <u>'second-draft'</u> activity. Get stuff down in the first draft; get pruning in the second. What should you look to cut out?

Obviously, those <u>three big monsters:</u>**ambiguity, repetition and jargon.**

Dull adjectives don't do this job. They are clichéd.

A tautology says the same thing twice, as in wet water, new innovation etc.

Clichés are weary old phrases that everyone knows and which tell us nothing new.

Be funny—if you know it will work

People like humour, and if you can make them laugh gently, then you'll be even more of a pleasure to read.

Riders

☞ You must know your audience...

☞ ... and know that they find you funny. Sadly, some people think they are funny but just aren't. If you're not getting the laughs, then cut the comedy.

☞ The most effective humour to use is that directed at oneself, or, at the other extreme, at the general ironies of life. Laughs at the expense of any social group, race or nationality will probably cause offence, and are best avoided.

Be original whenever you can

The greatest aid to originality is the drafting process. It helps you to be original in <u>two stages.</u>

In your <u>first draft,</u> you can experiment. In the <u>second draft,</u> if you feel the experiment hasn't worked, you can remove it.

> *NOTE:* Re-reading may show you have copied something direct from another source or that you unintentionally sound like someone else's writing.

How one develops the writing style is a mysterious process. This happens over time: the more you write, and read, the more you develop your own 'voice'. You have to allow yourself to experiment in order for this process to occur.

Practise

Anyone who is good at anything practises.

Lively writing

- ☞ Use the active voice, not the passive.
- ☞ Use positive verbs, not negative ones.
- ☞ Be as specific as you can.
- ☞ Keep learning new words.
- ☞ Use simile, metaphor and analogy.
- ☞ Be assertive.
- ☞ Be funny—if you know it will work.
- ☞ Be original whenever you can.
- ☞ Practise!

VII. Sentences and Paragraph

But there is more to style than this; style is also about crafting sentences and paragraphs.

Complex Sentences

As kids, we probably all wrote essays that followed the pattern below:

What we did on our holidays by Kapish.

We packed our cases. We got in the car. We drove to Jim Corbett sanctuary. Nikita was sick twice. We parked outside the hotel. We went in. A man in a cap stuck a piece of paper on our window. Daddy had an argument with him. The man telephoned the police. Two policemen came to see us.

And so on...*Strings of simple sentences.* As we got older, our style improved and we made the sentences more complex, by:

☞ using conjunctions
- We packed our cases and got in the car.

☞ using colons or semicolons
- We drove to Jim Corbett sanctuary; Nikita was sick twice.

☞ creating subordinate clauses
- When a man in a cap stuck a piece of paper on our window, Daddy had an argument with him.

You might also include a fragment to make a particular section vivid:
- Nikita was sick. Twice.

Let's say a grown-up version becomes:

We packed our cases, got in the car and drove to Jim Corbett Sanctuary. Nikita was sick—twice. We parked outside the hotel and went in. A man in a peaked cap stuck a piece of paper on our window. Daddy had an argument with him. The man telephoned the police, and two officers came to see us...

In writing the above the following was done:

☞ Bundled dull but necessary information into single sentence for example, sentence one gets us to Jim Corbett Sanctuary.
☞ Kept more interesting sentences solitary, to heighten their effect
☞ Expanded one simple sentence with the semi-comic dash.

A danger with complex sentences is that they become too complex, and the reader gets lost. Apparently the average sentence length in professionally written non-fiction material is 17 words.

Two particular problems in over-long sentences are webs of subordinate clauses and strings of 'ands'.

Subordinate clause overload

A basic rule in sentence construction is to get the subject, the main verb on to the page quickly, so the reader knows what the sentence is about and what sort of action we are talking about. You can get to the object quickly, too, that's an added bonus; have our basic picture in place, and can now elaborate on it certain amount of comfort.

Strings of ands

The innocuous conjunction and can land poor writers in all kinds of mess. Here's a piece of writing:

Implementation of Strategy B will ensure consistency of

application <u>and</u> on-going improvements of processes <u>and</u> systems across process and business boundaries.

Look at the *ands*. What does the writer mean? It could be that the strategy will ensure three things:
- consistency of application
- on-going improvements of processes
- on-going improvements of systems all of these across process and business boundaries.

Or two things:
- consistency of application of processes and systems
- on-going improvements of processes and systems—both of these across two kinds of boundary, process and business.

Or even:
- consistency of application

and two other things:
- on-going improvements of processes
- on-going improvements of systems
- both of these across two kinds of boundary, process and business.

Or some other combination?

Assuming the middle one is correct, how could it be phrased better? One way is to use bullet points:

Implementation of Strategy B will ensure:
- consistency of application
- on-going improvements of processes and systems, across process and businessboundaries.

Alternatively, use the word *both*, plus a well-placed comma:

Implementation of Strategy B will ensure both

Consistency of application and on-going improvements of
Processes and systems, across process and business boundaries

Of course, the language remains obscure and flabby. But at least the sentence now has a proper, unambiguous shape.

Here is another example:

Rita had the most beautiful eyes I had ever seen, black hair and a smile that was joyful and life enhancing and I fell in love with her in five minutes.

This is overloaded with *ands*: How do we get round this?
It is a bit unromantic to use bullet points:

Rita had:

☞ the most beautiful eyes I had ever seen
☞ black hair
☞ a smile that was joyful and life-enhancing
and I fell in love with her in five minutes

Though at least if we did that the sentence would be clear. So what can we do?

Back to basics: first, find the pivot of the sentence—obviously, here, it's before and I. So let's put a break in here. A semicolon? Go further, and split the sentence into two,

- Rita had the most beautiful eyes I had ever seen, black hair and a smile that was joyful and life-enhancing. I fell in love with her in five minutes.

Let's remove this potent confusion by using both:

Rita had the most beautiful eyes I had ever seen, black hair and a smile that was both joyful and life-enhancing. I fell in love with her in five minutes.

Five minutes? It took that long?

Perfect balance!

- The fairest part of the earth the most civilised portion of mankind . . .
- Ancient renown disciplined valour.

Both those contrasts pivot on the word *and*. Other conjunctions—but is the classic one—'contrasting balance' : (She was poor but she was honest.)

A contrasting balance doesn't have to have conjunctions: it can pivot around a colon or semicolon.

- A former writing student sent a programme she'd written for an exhibition of some of her artwork. Her last sentence ran:
  The paintings *on show* here are in bright, clear colours, the *colour of happy* dreams: my nightmares I keep in the *portfolio*.

The opposite of balanced writing is, rather obviously, imbalanced writing.

Imbalanced writing can be unclear:

- At the animal shelter we found black cats and dogs.

Black cats and black dogs, or black cats and dogs of all sort of colours? Answer, probably, the former. But probably enough readers don't want 'probably'; <u>they want clarity.</u>

- At the animal shelter we found dogs and black cats.

This will do it. Better still, because more equally balanced, is:

- At the animal shelter we found dogs of all colourings and black cats.

Dogs of all colourings → black cats

This has a noun and an adjective (or adjective phrase) on each of the balance. Note that in this example, the balancing pairs been 'switched round'.

☞ Noun (dogs) + adjective - adjective (black) + noun
☞ phrase (of all colours) (cats).

This is a neat and very old trick, technically called **'chiasmus'**

If you want to stress that you were looking for a marmalade cat and were disappointed, then use a contrasting balance and write:

- At the animal shelter we found dogs of all colourings but only black cats.

Ending Sentences Effectively

The standard wisdom is that the <u>beginning of a sentence sets the scene.</u>

<u>The end is where you 'pay off'</u> the sentence by making your most <u>emphatic comment.</u>

- Climate change will cause flooding and other forms of land degradation, bringing about massive economic disruption, involuntary migration and probably the deaths of millions of people.

Your writing will become predictable and dull. The end of a sentence can be a good place to set up a link to the next sentence.

Paragraphs

As with sentences, the topic of a paragraph should usually be a noun at the beginning. It doesn't have to be the first word—though often is, example in a heading. But after the first sentence of a paragraph, reader should be thinking, 'This paragraph is about this topic.'

Paragraphs will have a build-up in the early sentences leading the key point around the middle. Just as with sentences, the end of the paragraph is a place for maximum emphasis.

Unity

Poor paragraphs stray off the point. They do this because half through the paragraph the writer is reminded of something interesting to say. This is, after all, what we often do in conversation. And, actually, first draft, it's not a bad thing to do, as it can open up new perspectives. The failure lies in not editing the paragraph later: the interest digression needs to be taken back under the writer's control.

For example:
☞ A woman who was tall and in a green saree saw the accident.
☞ The surrender of the man before the court is probably more interesting than the facts. We are breaking a promise to the reader.
☞ Clarity is missing!

Using Passives for Unity

Consider this passage:

The next stop on our journey is Shimla. Shimla was the favourite place for Lord Dalhousie. "Balls here and balls there" he'd say. He refers to the game of golf.

If it is more united, more under control then the sentence subjects are now the next stop.

Bad writing often just leaps from one idea to another, leaving the reader lost and wondering what on earth has happened.

Metadiscourse

Though a paragraph introduces a new topic or viewpoint, it's still nice to be led gently into it. 'Metadiscourse', odd words or phrases like *however, moreover, on the other hand* that often begin paragraphs, relating them back to what the reader has read and teeing them up for what's going to come.

Informal numbering is metadiscourse. The writer says: There are four reasons why the India should embrace the financial liberation. Then he gives the four reasons, each one having its own paragraph. Try and vary your metadiscourse here:

Don't just say First, Secondly... Thirdly... Fourthly... at the start of each respective paragraph. If you just once say something like A third reason is... you've livened things up enormously. Most important of all, please make sure you pay off the promise. The number of times we read pieces that talk about, say, 'five factors and begin by enumerating them (The first is... Secondly...) then we leave readers to search around for the other three. It's disgusting!

Simply use headings. These tell the reader clearly and simply that the old topic is done and a new one about to begin. They also tell the reader what that new topic is going to be.

They help you to organise your thoughts, and your readers organise theirs. They inspire confidence in your readers-you are in control of their journey from being uninformed to being informed.

Paragraphs

Focus

☞ Make the paragraph about something

- ☞ Tell the reader early on what the paragraph is about
- ☞ Don't wander off the subject
- ☞ Keep the sentences united!
- ☞ Keep the subjects of most sentences related to the paragraph topic
- ☞ Use passives, if necessary
- ☞ Flow, don't jump—make the necessary links between thoughts
- ☞ Use 'metadiscourse' to fill in the gaps between paragraph
- ☞ Vary paragraph lengths
- ☞ Three to six sentences is average

Paragraph length

As with sentences, keep paragraph lengths varied. Most paragraphs in professionally written work are between three and six sentence long. What is undoubted is paragraphs have been getting shorter in modern writing especially in advertising.

Sections

Sections are the next level up from paragraphs. In essence the rules are similar to those for paragraphs:
- ☞ make them about something
- ☞ tell the reader clearly and quickly what they are about
- ☞ don't wander off the subject
- ☞ keep a natural flow going.

The good writer consciously varies the length of paragraphs and sentences, but not of sections. However well-balanced pieces of work have sections of similar lengths.

How sections fit together is essentially a matter of structure.

VIII. Audience, Planning, Structure

So let us get to the very act of writing.

First of all, you need to think about your audience and to do some planning. So
- Think 'reader'
- Plan

Think 'reader'

People at the receiving end of what you are communicating; if they don't understand what you are trying to say, your attempt at communication has failed, however brilliant you thought it was.

So, the first question you must ask yourself is, 'Who is going read this?'

'Lots of different people' is not a good enough answer. If answer is a lot of people, then ask yourself <u>what they have in common.</u>

<u>Think like a marketer: SEGMENTING:</u> If their audience is a divided one, marketers subdivide them into meaningful sub-groups; then aim subtly different communications at each sub-group.
- A manual for a new piece of software for a bank will only be read by employees of that bank, and only by employees at a certain level.
- A sales report might be aimed at members of a board.
- A piece in the film magazine is for film buffs. Yes, you may say, but 'film buffs' means everyone from academicians to sportspersons.

> *NOTE:* Having segmented their audience, marketers often go on to imagine an ideal model listener, an 'archetype'. You should do the same.

Imagine the archetype actually reading what you have written. Ask some questions.

Have you got credibility with this person?

- Good. Don't waste it. Having credibility will make this reader give you a little more time, but if you start boring them, then that advantage will soon be lost.
- You need to establish it, fast. Readers need to know- they need to know it quickly, or they are lost.

<u>If you're writing a letter,</u> explain why you are writing to that person. The explanation needs to be centred round your perception of the reader's needs and interests, not your needs interests. Every reader asks, 'What's in it for me?'

If the reader is an acquaintance, remind them of your point of contact.

What does the reader know already?

This is crucial. Who is that person.

What does the reader need to know?

In any workplace document, this question is crucial. Outside the workplace, you can relax a little, and simply ask, 'What would the reader like to know?'

'What do I want to tell them?' don't try to impress; try to express.

- What has been achieved (not how it was done)

☞ **Important**: How much time does the reader have for my communication?

Assume there is less time than you think.

Don't follow the adage:'I'm sorry to write such a long letter: I didn't have time to write a short one.'

Keep your reader in mind as you write and as you re-write. <u>The Golden Rule</u>—every word should lead your reader forward. Not just any old reader, but yours...

Beware: There is the Thinking 'Reader'

- Who is going to read this?
  - imagine an 'archetype'
- Have I got credibility with this person?
- What is their level of technical knowledge?
- What do they need to know?
  - or, away from work, what would they like to know?
- How much time do they have to attend to me?
- Keep the reader in mind throughout the writing process.

Planning

Start with the basics.
- What is your piece about?
- What's its message?

Structure

There are <u>two basic structures</u>—narrative and aspect-by-aspect.

<u>Simple narrative</u> is the best way of ensuring a piece flows: Tell me a story our children ask from a very early age. This happened; then that happened; then that happened. Beginning, middle and end.

If you are describing long, complex processes, think of how you can break these down into phases or stages—groups of naturally related actions that occur reasonably closely together in time. These will be the sections of the piece.

Let us look at the process of doing a commercial deal; it could be broken down into:

☞ Initial contact
☞ Testing how serious both sides are
☞ Producing an outline agreement
☞ Building trust
☞ Negotiating detail
☞ Last-minute problems
☞ Signing.

We can order them sequentially:
☞ Order them by starting time
☞ Explain where they overlap
☞ If the overlaps are complex, use a bar diagram to illustrate them.

The other basic structure for looking at a topic is aspect-by-aspect.

When planning to present material aspect-by-aspect is a 'mini map'; it is hugely useful. Put the subject at the centre of the page, I imagine various aspects radiating out from it like spokes from hub.

For example, buying a house… the market, the schools next door, shopping malls, banks etc.

Remember Kipling's Six Wise Men

I keep six honest serving-men
(They taught me all I knew);
Their names are **What** and **Why** and **When**
And **How** and **Where** and **Who**.

The **mind-map** into a plan for a piece of writing, put the aspects in an order that readers will find useful. Unless otherwise instructed, they will assume that the first point you make is the most important one. Use this, or tell the reader that you are going to list the aspects in some other order, such as cost. Don't waste the opportunity to pass information to the reader by just placing things in random order.

Remember 'To fail to prepare is to prepare to fail'.:
☞ THESIS: the issue
☞ ANTI-THESIS: the opposite argument (the 'antithesis')
☞ SYNTHESIS: And finally your view (the 'synthesis') is.

If many thesis' work through the:

Sequentially
☞ Thesis
☞ Antithesis A
☞ Comments on Antithesis A
☞ Antithesis B
☞ Comments on Antithesis B
☞ Antithesis C
☞ Comments on Antithesis C
☞ Your: Synthesis.

A business report structure:
☞ Current problem
☞ Initial attempts at solving it, and why they failed
☞ Proposed new solution
☞ Implications of new solution for various parts of the business/other relevant parties
☞ Any objections, and how they will be met
☞ Specific actions required of individual people/ departments
☞ Present a picture of what things will be like when the new solution is put into practice successfully

Once you have thought through your overall plan, you really are ready to get writing!

Planning your piece

• Theme	What's your piece about?
• Structure	Narrative
• Phases	Aspect-by-aspect
• Make a mind-map	Dialectic

Work through the theses and antitheses.

IX. The Actual Process

You've laid out the basic plan for the piece—what it's about, what you're going to say about this topic. You know how you're going to structure your presentation of the material. Now it is time to go ahead!

The Process

Begin by writing a 'skeleton' outline.

It's amazing how arguments can look finepaper, but suddenly feel inadequate when spoken out loud.

If you do give the talk live, take note of any criticisms made.

There are various possibilities
☞ The critic is right—you're wrong.
☞ The critic is right, given their perspective, but this perspective isn't yours or your target audience's.

The critic just has a different belief. On most subjects worth discussing, there are competing views.

The critic is simply wrong.

Don't be swayed by critics without thinking which of the above categories they belong to.

A positive comment is often a lead-in to something a person wants to say about their own experience—so let them tell the tale, and take note of it. Have a chat with them after the talk if you can. But at the same time, don't be swayed into thinking you now have the absolute truth! Think carefully about how these new comments illustrate or expand what you have to say, and build these new insights into the talk where relevant.

'The building of our success is often built by the stones hurled at us by others.'

Now it's time to do some real writing, as you 'flesh out' this skeleton, turning it into the first full draft.

The ideal way to write a first draft is to sit down with your revised skeleton plan, start writing, write to the end, then finish.

Remember different people draft differently.

☞ Some write, as recommended, straight through, beginning to end.
☞ Others pause mid-way and edit what has been written.
☞ Good sentences are not written; they are often re-written!

You can always re-draft and re-write.

In defence of pausing midway, then editing, priorities change you write. Stuff that looked like it belonged in one section suddenly seems to belong somewhere else.

Early the first drafting process, you can go back and edit. But I give yourself a deadline though.

This <u>first draft</u> then needs to be reviewed, ideally after some kind of break.

Some believe that 'creative' writing must put a draft aside for three months—not a possibility for most of us. But at least give it some time. Print out a copy, pick up a red pen, and go through it quickly, noting with a mark in the margin any bits that:

☞ read badly
☞ fail to make sense
☞ are boring, or
☞ don't say what you thought they would say.

Then, at the end of your read-through, close your eyes and try and think holistically. Overall, does the piece say:
- ☞ what you want to say
- ☞ in the way you want to say it
- ☞ to the people you are communicating with?

The key question is: Did the arguments flow logically? Were there steps missing? Was all the relevant information present? Note down your thoughts.

Now work through the piece again. Sort out the big problems first—the high-level re-write. Fill in any gaps in the argument. Is all the material in the right place?

Make various versions of your document.

One of the most difficult tasks in revising is taking out matter especially if you put a lot of effort into it, or, hardest of all.

When you have made all the necessary changes, you effectively have a second full draft. As with the first one, leave it for a bit, then re-visit. Hopefully, it will be much tighter, better focused and read better than your first version.
- ☞ What is the piece about and what do you want to say about this?
- ☞ Plan.
- ☞ Write a first draft.
- ☞ Put this aside; re-think! 'Re-visit and revise' is of huge value.

Fonts

Please use standard, readable typefaces (or 'fonts'). There are basically three types:
- Those with 'serifs': A serif is a tiny embellishment to the basic letter shape that makes the letter easier to

recognise. This, of course, makes the text easier to read, and thus helps the brain get into a 'flow' state, so use these for your basic text. Times New Roman is the classic one.
- Fonts without serifs, known as sans-serif. Sans-serif fonts like Helvetica and Anal are often used in headings, to create variety when the main text is in a serif font—though we use Times New Roman both for headings and main text, and it looks fine to most!

NOTE: Some people believe that sans-serif fonts are easier to read off computer screens which is why the default font for the emails you receive is Anal.

- Novelty fonts. These are avoided in any serious communication, and to be used sparingly in humorous ones.

Different fonts work best in different sizes (also called 'points') 11- or 12-point Times New Roman produces a nice, readable page; 10-point is a bit small, and 14 too clumsy.

Headings

Think through your 'hierarchy of headings'.

A short, one-page document might have the main heading 14-point bold and the rest of the text in 12 or 11-point.

Justification

JUSTIFICATION means having straight lines at both the left and right margins of the text. All text should be 'left-hand justified', which means nice straight line down the left-hand side of the text. Proper books have nice straight lines left and right, which creates authoritative looking blocks of text.

The drawback to this is that because you've had to fit the text into what is effectively a box, you end up with the spacing between words being different on different lines—some lines look all bunched up, others look all stretched out, which is tiring on the eye. Professionally printed books get round this by various subtle techniques, including hyphenating words at line-ends to keep a consistent average number of letters (or spaces or punctuation marks) per line. You haven't the time to do this (or the skill: typesetters know where to hyphenate a word to stop it looking silly). Left-hand justify only.

Writing as a Group or Pair

Many documents are written by groups of people. Someone needs to be in charge, and have the role of editor. This can be a demanding job. This person needs:
- to be a good writer
- to have adequate technical knowledge of the subject
- diplomacy
- firmness
- the ability to inspire and motivate the rest of the team.
- The team need to agree the basic points, then brainstorm mind-map (and any pruning of the mind-map).
- The team leader should then draw up the skeleton outline, which should be circulated and agreed.
- Then the leader must allocate sections to relevant people, who then go off and write first drafts by agreed dates.
- The leader should then gather these, chasing any late submitters, turn them all into a first full draft of the

document. This will almost undoubtedly involve some editing.
- ☞ Contributors will inevitably complain about this: the leader should listen carefully, in case it is some necessary technical subtlety that has been edited out. By the end, the editor's decision is final.
- ☞ This first full draft should be circulated, and the team should try to discuss.
- ☞ Any re-writing is submitted to the leader, who then produce second draft, which is circulated.
- ☞ A final meeting, and then he goes away, makes any changes he or she thinks fit, then circulates.

The document is ready for all contributors for them to 'sign off'.

This model is rather undemocratic, but pieces written by groups with no one in charge lack authority.

Smaller joint documents can be passed round electronically and have attributed comments left on them. But, as always, someone must be responsible for the end product, and that someone must have the final say in which changes are accepted and which rejected.

It's quite common to write as a pair—a subject-matter expert and a professional writer.

There are three keys to making this relationship work:
- ☞ Find someone you like.
- ☞ Find someone who already has some knowledge of, and, more important, an interest in, your subject.
- ☞ Be clear from the outset about the nature and details of your cooperation.

You will need to be clear from the outset about issues such as:

☞ Confidentiality. The writer must agree to this.
☞ Time and money. The writer must be paid.
☞ Attribution. Will the piece be 'ghosted' (just the expert's name on the cover, with a 'thank you' in the foreword) or fully authored?
☞ Ownership. Co-authored works should, rather obviously, be the copyright of both authors.

Team authorship is not easy, but can work when the above rules are followed.

X. Specific Writing Situations

Email

Email is probably the most common form of written communication now. When it was first being widely used, email was thought of as a kind of instant letter, but now it has developed its own characteristics, distinct from phone conversations or letters.

EMAIL

- Informal
- Written
- Arrives quickly
- Read or answered at once
- Keep it brief!
- Easy to copy to many people
- Waits to be read
- Poor security

PHONE

- Informal
- Verbal
- Instant
- Can be a nice long chat
- One-to-one
- Intrusive—answer me now!
- Poor security

LETTER

- Formal
- Takes time to arrive
- Usually one-to-one
- Security better
- Written
- Can be longer
- Waits to be read

If it's like any pre-existing medium, email is like the postcard.

Email is best used for simple things—a question, an answer question. Even with longer emails, try and fit them on to the F that appears when you click them open, which allows for lines of text.

How should emails be written?

The answer: CORRECTLY.

☞ There's no excuse for bad grammar or punctuation.
☞ There is no excuse for failure to think through and have clarity of material.

☞ IMPORTANT: There is no excuse for rubbish spelling, as all email systems have a spellchecker.

Where an email has serious content—first have it as a Word document, then paste it into the email. Having done this, re-read it and allow for small changes—sometimes phrases that sound fine in the Word document look a bit stiff and formal when ready to be sent off as email.

And, of course, remember the adage, **'Email in haste, repent at leisure'!**

It's very easy to bash out an email when in a powerful fleeting mood and fire it off in the heat of the moment to who has got you into this mood. Unwise. Think before you click. Better still, store it in the draft folder and don't send it till the morning.

Whatever kind of email you are writing, **layout is important:** reading from a screen is harder than reading from paper.

☞ Use short paragraphs and leave blank lines between them.
☞ Don't go in for fancy formatting, as some recipients' machines can't handle this.
☞ 'Upgrade' emails to html, which allows you to use italics and put the other person's email replies in blue if replying paragraph by paragraph.
☞ There's a debate about how to begin emails:
  - Dear—sounds a bit formal;
  - Hi—sounds a bit casual;
  - Just the person's name sounds a bit peremptory.
  - With people I don't know we use Dear—.
  - With people we get into the habit of using 'Hi—which is fine as long as the email is friendly rather than critical
  - If it's critical, we tend to revert to 'Dear—'.

In the end, you have to work out what suits you.

The same goes for **signing off.** Letters had nice clear rules; email doesn't…

The **'subject' box is important,** especially if you are emailing people you don't know; as this is what they will see before deciding to open it. If you are writing on a personal recommendation, mention that person in the subject box. If not, then pick out what is it about your email that will be of interest to them.

Email Etiquette

There is quite a lot of material around about EMAIL ETIQUETTE, all of it largely agreed:
- Don't use capitals or '!!!'
- Don't attach documents unless requested to.
  - Stay in the 'thread' (in other words, click 'Reply' not 'New' when answering someone's email, which will mean that all the previous correspondence gets sent back with your reply).
  - Don't send on chain letters.
  - Answer quickly—within 24 hours.
  - Don't expect instant replies: if a message is really urgent: get on the phone.
  - Do answer all the questions asked in an email.
  - Contact the recipient again when that time is up.
  - Don't overuse the red 'urgent' exclamation mark.
  - Don't spam, or semi-spam. Write emails to actual people.
  - If, for some reason, you do get 'flamed' (sent an abusive email) by someone, don't get into an argument.

Memoranda

'Memos' are often sent via email, but deserve a brief mention of their own. As with emails, they should be brief and to the point. Head them with the basics: from, to, date, subject. For the actual text, this three-section model covers most memos:
- Problem
- Solution
- Specific action(s). What do you want the recipient to do? What are you intending to do or what have you done?

Instructions

The number one rule for instructions is to think 'reader'. Ideally, you should talk to users and find out which aspects they find, or found, difficult. If a machine/piece of software/procedure is totally new. Let potential users try it. Watch what they do, talk with them as they do it, and be brief afterwards.

If this is not possible, think hard about 'segmenting':

☞ What sort of person will be following the instructions?
☞ What level of technical knowledge will they have?

The answer to the last question is usually 'less than you think': If in doubt, imagine your instructions being read by a person who is of average intelligence but who has no technical knowledge at all.

10 key points for creating good instructions:

☞ Take the user step by step through all the main procedures.
☞ If the process is at all interactive—e.g. with a machine—don't just say what the user should do, but say what the machine will do in response. Turn machine on.
☞ Again, for a machine, list, and ideally show in a picture, all the component parts and describe what they do.
☞ For software, show the main screens that the user will see.
☞ List common user mistakes.
☞ Have a 'troubleshooting' section.
☞ For a long set of instructions, list contents at the front and a thorough index at the back.
☞ If you send someone somewhere with instructions make sure those instructions can be carried out.
☞ Don't be afraid to over-explain.
☞ Use imperatives—open the lid—rather than passives

Remember that technical vocabulary doesn't just mean well.

Advertisements

Any ad is a process, taking the reader through a journey which begins by trying to get them noticing the ad and ends with them taking the action they want them to.

This formula is **AIDA**:
- **Attention**
- **Interest**
- **Desire**
- **Action**

Attention is usually drawn by a picture or a simple heading in large print. The picture or heading should be relevant. We all leap at the word FREE!

Interest is aroused by readers perceiving that the ad relates to them and their interests in a specific way. Best of all, the ad relates to a problem they currently have.

Desire means, obviously, that readers are no longer just interested by, but actually want, your 'offer' (whatever you are advertising). Getting them to this state involves at least three steps (which is where the complications to the AIDA acronym come in). You must:

Action means, explain how your offer solves their problem/satisfies their want. Convince them that it will work. Convince them that it will work for them.

Sales Letters

These should be written with the same **AIDA** process in mind.

There are two types of sales letter:
☞ One is a specific one to people with whom you are acquainted (i.e. whom you have met, but don't know that

well). The key obstacle to overcome here is to remind them of that acquaintance. Once they say, 'Oh, yes, I remember then you have credibility and can get on with the interest, the **action**!

☞ Two: For letters to people unknown to you—for example, people selected from mailing lists—the key is in the 'headline'.

Take time crafting the headline. Try various alternatives. Get other people to look at the various versions and see which one works for them.

Remember the rule: Think 'reader'.

Reports

Reports also need 'topping and tailing'—*topping* with a powerful summary, and *tailing* with an index, so readers can come back to sections with ease and confidence, and sometimes references.

☞ Many people say that the summary is the most important of a report. It is certainly the most read part—so you must get your main points into it. Some of you might object that this takes the interest out of the rest of it, a bit like prefacing a 'who did it'.

☞ The job of the report is to back up the conclusions presented in the summary with detailed arguments, facts and figures.

The summary must be in plain language, and should only be one page long. It must cover:

☞ The problem
☞ Your recommended solution
☞ The main implications of that solution (cost, time etc.).

The summary is sometimes called an **'executive summary'**.

Indexing is largely a matter of thoroughness.

Referencing is often important in reports—those readers who get beyond the summary may well want to check your facts and/or quotes, so provide references for them to do so.

Business Plans

These are similar to reports, in that the summary is by far the most important section, and the rest of the plan is simply back-up-for that important first page.

There are plenty of model business plans available, free, on internet. Use one as a template, and remember to avoid management in your writing!

Business Letters

The basic rules of good writing matter.
- Use ordinary, not pompous words.
- Be ruthless in checking for, and removing, ambiguity—both actual and potential, remember.

<u>Your letter should fit on to a page.</u>
The old rules for ending letters were:
- If you addressed the letter to an individual, Dear Ms. Smith, you ended 'Yours sincerely'.
- If you addressed the letter Dear Sir/Madam, then you ended 'Yours faithfully'.

Now, our computer tells us to end, *Yours truly*.

General Interest Pieces

Remember the question 'What's the piece about?' Well-known people can get away with a series of rambling thoughts on life, the universe and everything; the rest of us can't, and need to be saying something specific to merit taking up readers' time and attention.

Remember to find out from the medium where your piece may appear and how many words they want—and stick to that figure.

Web Pages

People read web copy more slowly than they do paper copy. They are also more impatient. As a result, you have to grab the visitor's attention quickly and make sure that you keep it. A few specialist web points are worth noting, however:

- Research shows that many readers don't scroll, so get all information on to one screen.
- Every page should have a 'headline' to grab the attention of the surfer. These should be simple and factual.
- As with email, use short sentences and short paragraphs. Have space between the paragraphs.
- Use highlighted words but don't overload your text with them. One or two per paragraph is ideal.

> *NOTE:* hyperlinks (those underlined words you click on that take you automatically to another page) can double as highlighted words.

- Use headings.
- Use bullet points.
- Use sans-serif typefaces.

The nature of hyperlinks has altered the way pieces of writing are structured on the web. A ten-page document should be down to a one-page summary, with hyperlinks on each main aspect so that readers who want to investigate that aspect more deeply can click and be taken to a secondary, specialist page.

PowerPoint Slides

As with all communication, keep these simple. The ideal PowerPoint slide has a heading and three or four bulleted points. Have more consideration for your audience!

Multicultural Muddle

Here is as passage, from an advertisement for a Deputy Director of Social Services, is a real polysyllabic mess.

Multicultural urban environment, despite modern delicacies, simply means racially mixed part of town. Integrate here may mean build or it may have been misused to mean include:

Experience of managing a multicultural urban environment and the ability to integrate equalities considerations into areas of work activity.

Every trade and profession is entitled to its own jargon— up to a point so that it allows equalities and is readily understood among social services people as meaning equal treatment regardless of race, sex and, probably, physical handicaps—although the singular equality serves the purpose as well, or better.

That passage, converted into plain English, could read:

Experience of dealing with a racially mixed town area and ability to ensure that equality is part of departmental life.

The same advertisement also required ability to organise intervention in the community; to establish the needs of potential service users meaning, presumably, ability to go out to discover what people need us to do.

Social workers do not have the field to themselves when it comes to jargon.

An advertisement for a health worker announced:

You will assist the team in formulating and implementing a health policy, evaluating and developing appropriate responses to specific health problems in indigenous areas.
Meaning?

If we try to translate this: *You will help to plan and carry out a policy to deal with health problems among local people.*

Such a simplification may create a problem, however; to jargon-hardened health workers the revised job description sounds as though it's less important and so worth only half the salary of the inflated version.

Computerspeak and Psychobabble

We can no longer ignore the jargon that computers have generated as computing has evolved from cult to mass culture. Even quite young children are now familiar with many of the terms: *floppy, prompt, menu, boot, megahertz, toolbar, drag* and *drop* hold no terrors for them. However, some of the worst offences against the English language pour in an unending stream from the computer world:

Driven and focused by seeing the world from the customer's perspective, we continue to build an organisation where quality is embedded in every aspect of endeavour . . . our continued growth in the network computing industry mandates that we now identify and attract the most talented and creative sales and marketing professionals.

This announcement sounds as if it were written by someone whose dictionary had a yellow stained pages on the relevant entry.

Is writing jargon and management-speak more difficult than writing plain English? Many examples suggest that it is, yet its devotees persist in working harder than they need to.

Notice this job description in an advertisement for a XYZ Company position:

The XYZ Company seeks a Human Resources Assessment Technologist, Corporate Management Development.

But jargonising also offers a lazy way out.

Notice a press release about forthcoming conference which deserves full marks for laziness:

Conjoint Family Therapy, demonstration/participation workshop. This is a demonstration/participation workshop illustrating 20 to 30 'ways of being' as therapist i.e. 'self as instrument'/strategies/techniques) presented from an experiential-Gestalt/communications skills/learning theory/ whatever else philosophical viewpoint. Emphasis is on experiencing... family/therapist/ participant/self, the several modalities, strategies, values, processes, procedures, goals, dangers, fears, avoidance, growth and excitement of conjoint interaction.

Euphemism

Euphemisms—words and phrases people use to avoid making a statement that is direct, clear and honest—are often used out of kindness when the direct expression might give needless offence.

That's the trouble with euphemisms—they tend to be self-defeating because they paint a thick coat over clarity and understanding.

For example a deaf person is often described as *hard of hearing* and a *part-blind* person as partially sighted. Unfortunately, in recent times these traditional and harmless euphemisms have been extended and replaced with such terms as aurally or *visually challenged*.

Have you ever admitted that you might have been, well, to put it bluntly—drunk? How often have you heard someone honestly admit they were drunk? : No, they might admit to having been *one over the eight*, *high-spirited*, *happy*, *a bit merry*, but drunk—never!

Any user of the English language has to become something of an expert in understanding the true meaning of euphemisms, so much are they a part of our everyday lives.

We need these seemingly innocent terms as replacements for those that are embarrassing, unpleasant, crude or offensive.

Our euphemistic skills are honed by the media which, though much franker nowadays, still maintain some taboo areas:

- *intimacy* occurred (had sex);
- she was *strangled and mutilated* but had not been interfered with (killed but not raped);
- *abused* (today's vague catch-all euphemism for any form of questionable physical, psychological or sexual activity).
- It is, as you can see, a very short journey from *sex-change operation* to *gender reassignment*.

The language of prudery also surprisingly invades that sanctum of directness, the doctor's surgery.
☞ The *poor*, in our euphemistic world, are in a *lower income bracket, underprivileged* or *fiscal under-achievers*.
☞ Slum homes are *inner-city housing*.
☞ When a city decides to clear away the slums the process is called *urban renewal* rather than slum clearance. And of course the same city calls its *rat catchers rodent operatives*.

Death has no dearth of euphemisms.
☞ Shakespeare might well ask today, 'Death, where is thy sting?'
☞ Senior Citizens and Golden Agers no longer simply die, *they pass on, pass away, depart, sleep with the angels, go to their just reward, go to a better place, take a last bow, answer the final call, pop off, go on a final journey, fade away* or, more jocularly, *kick the bucket*.

Euphemism is particularly effective for disguising crime—especially the crimes we might commit ourselves:
☞ Tax fiddling
☞ meter feeding
☞ fare dodging, joy
☞ streetwise skills, i.e cheating and criminal activity.

<u>Euphemism is also useful to help to make tedious-sounding jobs seem grand.</u>

Those people we used to know as **insurance salesmen** are now variously *financial advisers, investment consultants, fiscal analysts, savings strategists, liquidity planners pensions counsellors and endowments executives*.

Again, the euphemistic traps are laid early in the career paths of young people.

Job descriptions and what, in real working life, they probably mean:

Pleasant working manner essential:
- Must be subservient
- All the advantages of a large company
- Nobody knows anyone else's name
- Perfect opportunity for school leavers
- Pathetically low pay
- Salary negotiable
- But only downwards
- Earn money at home
- Be exploited under your own roof
- Earn service charge!
- But only through commission
- Must have a sense of humour
- Must not be a complainer.

Conclusion: 10 Commandments

- Think 'reader'.
- Plan.
- The Golden Rule: every word should lead your reader forward.
- Seek out, and eliminate, all ambiguity, actual or potential.
- In complex sentences, get subject, verb, object down as quickly as possible.
- Use variety and balance.
- Give your paragraphs both unity and flow.
- Clarity, clarity, clarity.
- Remember—you are being creative.
- Good sentences are not written; they are re-written.

Pitfalls
(Pitfalls of Style)

I. Avoid: Circumlocution

Circumlocution (also called **periphrasis**) typically employs long words, often incorrectly or inappropriately. This is done in order to sound learned :
- ☞ Not simply a bomb but an *explosive device*
- ☞ '*I wonder if you would mind awfully moving to one side*' instead of the more direct 'Get out of my way!'.
- ☞ NOTE: Some forms of circumlocution may be excusable, but most are due to unthinking use of jargon and clichés in place of more precise (and usually briefer) expressions:
- ☞ *exception of* for except;
- ☞ *with reference to*/regard to/respect to
- ☞ *for about*; for the very good reason that for because, and so on.

So stick to the point!
If you don't intend to drive from Delhi to Agra in the most direct way possible you'd hardly wander off every motorway, exit and then dither about along country lanes. <u>The same principle applies to effective communication.</u>

Circumlocutory phrases are uttered when the exact, simple word we want fails to turn up. Here's a short list.

The Circumlocutionist's Lexicon

apart from the fact that—but, except

as a consequence of—because of
as yet—yet
at the time of writing—now/at present
at this moment/point in time—now/at present
avail ourselves of the privilege—accept
be of the opinion that—think, believe
because of the fact that—because
beg to differ—disagree
by means of—by
by virtue of the fact that—because
consequent upon—because of
consonant with—agreeing/matching
could hardly be less propitious—is bad/unfortunate/unpromising
due to the fact that—because
during such time as—while
during the course of—during
except for the fact that—except/but
few in number—few
for the reason that/for the very good reason that—because
give up on (it)—give up
go in to bat for—defend/help/represent
in accordance with—under
in addition to which—besides
in a majority of cases—usually
in all probability—probably
in anticipation of—expecting
inasmuch as—since
in association with—with
in close proximity to—near
in connection with—about
in consequence of—because of
in contradistinction to—compared to/compared with

in excess of—over/more than
in isolation—alone
in less than no time—soon/quickly
in many cases/instances—often
in more than one instance—more than once
in order to—to
in respect of—about/concerning
in spite of the fact that—although/even though
in the absence of—without
in the amount of—for in the event that—if
in the light of the fact that—because
in the near future—soon
in the neighbourhood of/in the vicinity of—near/about
in the recent past—recently
in view of/in view of the fact that—because
irrespective of the fact that—although
large in size/stature—large/big
make a recommendation that—recommend that
nothing if not—very
notwithstanding the fact that—even if
of a delicate nature/character—delicate
of a high order—high/great/considerable
of the opinion that—think/believe
on account of the fact that—because
on a temporary basis—temporary/temporarily
on the grounds that—because
on the part of—by
owing to the fact that—because
pink/purple/puce, etc in colour—pink/purple/puce, etc
prior to—before
provide a contribution to—contribute to/help
regardless of the fact that—although
subsequent to—after

there can be little doubt that—no doubt, clearly
there is a possibility that—possibly/perhaps
to the best of my knowledge and belief—as far as I know/I believe
until such time as—until
with a view to—to
with reference to—about
with regard to—about
with respect to—about/concerning
with the exception of—except

AVOID pompous long-windedness.

Imagine the nursery rhyme 'three blind mice' re-written:

Observe repeatedly the precipitate progress of a trio of sightless rodents: together they coursed apace on the heels of the agriculturalist's consort, who summarily disjoined their caudal appendages with a cutler's handiwork. One had never witnessed such mirth in one's existence as the incident involving those hemeralopic and nyctalopic mammals. <u>The rhyme is, of course, 'Three Blind Mice'.</u>

II. Avoid: Tautology

Mr and Mrs Raul Francis are proud to announce the birth of a baby girl, Irene Agnes.

> *NOTE:* Now, like 'Dog Bites Man', this isn't really news. But what if Mrs Francis had given birth to an adult girl? That would be news! Obviously Mrs Francis had given birth to a baby; it happens all the time. The newsy bit is that it was a girl.

The use of the word *baby* here is what is known as **pleonasm,** the *use of redundant words*. The same would apply if Mrs Francis invited the neighbours in to see her 'new baby'. Are there any old babies? Of course all babies are new!

When a word repeats the meaning of another word in the same phrase it is called **tautology** and, usually, all verbal superfluities are known by this term:
- Free gift!
- Added extra!
- Added bonus!

> *NOTE:* These are exciting claims. And also wasted words: classic examples of tautology, the use of more than one word to convey the same thought.

A gift, if not free, is not a gift—except perhaps in the slang usage, 'That car was an absolute gift at ₹60,000'.

Something extra is clearly something added.

And a _bonus_ is normally an addition. Even if the word is used to describe something apart from money, an added bonus is an added addition.

We hear and read phrases howlers such as added bonus every day, from people who have not thought what they are saying or writing, or do not care.

So accustomed are we to **tautology** in everyday speech and reading that this form of language misuse can pass unnoticed:

☞ Will Singh's income be sufficient <u>enough</u> for you both?

How many of us would normally detect that enough is a wasted word?

Avoiding redundant words and expressions is a sign of a caring writer.

Here is an A to Z of some of the more **common superfluities.**

An A to Z of Tautology

absolute certainty
actual facts (and its cousin, true facts)
added bonus/extra
adequate/sufficient enough
a downward plunge
advance warning
appear on the scene
arid desert
attach together
audible click
burn down, burnt up (burn and burnt by themselves are usually better)
circle round, around

Little Red Book of Perfect Written English 75

collaborate together
connect together
consensus of opinion (it's simply consensus)
couple together
crisis situation
divide it up, divide off
each and every one
early beginnings
eat up
enclosed herewith, enclosed herein
end result
file away
final completion
final upshot
follow after
forward planning
free gift
funeral obsequies
future prospects
gather together
gale force winds
general consensus
grateful thanks
Have got (a common one, this. Simply have is fine)
the hoi polloi (as hoi means 'the', the is obviously redundant)
    hoist up
hurry up
important essentials
in between
inside of
indirect allusion
I saw it with my own eyes (who else's?)

join together
joint cooperation
just recently
lend out
link together
lonely isolation
meet together
merge together
mix together, mix things together
more preferable
mutual cooperation
necessary requisite
new beginner, new beginning
new creation
new innovation, new invention
original source
other alternative
outside of
over with (for ended, finished)
pair of twins
past history
penetrate into
personal friend
polish up
proceed onward
raze to the ground (raze by itself means exactly that)
really excellent
recall back
reduce down
refer back
relic of the past
renew again

repeat again
revert back
rise up
safe haven
seldom ever
set a new world record
settle up
sink down
still continue
sufficient enough
swallow down
this day and age
totally complete
totally finished
tiny little child
unique means the only one of its kind. You can't get much more unique than that.
Not even quite unique, absolutely unique and utterly unique
unexpected surprise
unite together
unjustly persecuted
usual habit
very pregnant
viable alternative
warm 75 degrees (of course 75 degrees is warm!)
whether or not
widow woman

There are *other forms of repetitions, some intentional and some not*.

Writers have often used it for effect, for example in Samuel Taylor Coleridge's *The Rime of the Ancient Mariner*:

Alone, alone, all, all alone,
Alone on a wide wide sea!

Or in this equally famous passage from a <u>speech of</u> Winston Churchill's:

We shall go on to the end, we shall <u>fight</u> in France, we shall <u>fight</u> on the seas and oceans, we shall fight with growing confidence and growing strength in the air, we shall defend our island, whatever the cost may be, we shall <u>fight</u> on the beaches, we shall <u>fight</u> on the landing grounds, we shall <u>fight</u> in the fields and in the streets, we shall <u>fight</u> in the hills; we shall never surrender.

Of course sometimes the rhetoric is powerful as in the "I have a dream" speech of Martin Luther King.

In writing, sometimes we have irritating repetitions as,
- 'Her opinion is, is that it will never work';
- 'The dealer admitted he had had the sideboard in his shop for two months';
- 'Not that that would bother her in the least.'

Take care with <u>double negatives,</u> relatives of pleonasm.

Double negatives often can leave the readers trying to work out what is meant, so they are probably best avoided.

III. Gobbledegook

ORIGIN of term 'Gobbledegook'

In 1944, a Texas congressman named Maury Maverick became so angry about the bloated bureaucratic language in memos he received that, he described it as **'gobbledegook'**.

Explaining the name he said it reminded him 'of an old turkey gobbler back in Texas that was always gobbledy-gobbling and strutting around with ludicrous pomposity. And at the end of this gobble-gobble-gobble was a sort of a gook'. Maverick was also the head of a federal agency and promptly issued an order to all his subordinates: 'Be short and say, what you are talking about. Let's stop pointing up programs, finalising contracts that stem from district, regional or Washington levels. No more patterns, effectuating, dynamics. Anyone using the words activation or implementation will be shot'.

Here's a compilation of witter words and phrases:

as it were
as such (as in according to the rules, as such, they do not preclude…)
absolutely (typically used instead of yes)
abundantly clear
actually
all things being equal
as a matter of fact
as far as I am concerned

as of right now
at the end of the day
at this moment in time
a total of (as in a total of forty-two applicants instead of forty-two applicants)
basically
by definition
by and large (has anyone ever worked out the meaning of this?)
currently
curiously enough
during the period from (instead of from January 16 to…)
each and every
existing
extremely
funnily enough (usually precedes something that is not funny at all)
good and proper
good and ready
having said that (get ready for the contradiction!)
I am here to tell you
I am of the opinion that
I am the first to admit (how can you be so sure?)
I have to say, here and now
if you like
in a manner of speaking
in due course
in other words
in point of fact
in the final analysis
in view of the fact that
it goes without saying that (but I'll say it anyway)
I would like to say (and I certainly will)

I would like to take this opportunity to
last but not least
let me just say, right here and now
let us just be clear about this
may I make so bold as to say
many a time; many's the time that
more than enough; more than a little
never cease to wonder
(to) name but a few
needless to say
no two ways about it
not to mention
obviously
oddly enough
of course
of necessity (instead of necessarily)
on the basis of
once and for all
one and the same
precious few
quite
quite simply
really
rest assured
say nothing of (as in to say nothing of last year's results…)
shall I say (as in it is, shall I say, a novel approach….)
so much the better, so much the worse
the fact of the matter: <u>The fact of the matter is, the Government is wrong…</u>
to all intents and purposes
to my mind, to one's own mind
to the point that

unless and until (as in unless and until they pay, they can't board the ship. Either word makes the necessary condition, so one of them is redundant.)

when all is said and done (not entirely meaningless but perhaps better replaced with still/however/nevertheless)

with all due respect, with the greatest respect

within the foreseeable future

Here's a sentence which includes three witter phrases:

<u>Needless to say,</u> we are, <u>if you like,</u> facing difficulties which, <u>when all is said and done</u>, we did not create ourselves.

Look at the sheer lack of meaning in these phrases:

☞ We are, *if you like*, facing difficulties which, *needless to say*, *when all is said and done*, we did not create ourselves.

Or

☞ *When all is said and done*, we are, *if you like*, facing difficulties which, *needless to say*, we did not create ourselves.

Without the witter words the sentence is more forceful, half as long, and has not lost any of its meaning:

☞ We are facing difficulties which we did not create ourselves.

The second ingredient of gobbledegook is waffle:
vague and wordy utterances that wander aimlessly along a path of meaning but effectively obscure it.

In its extreme form **logorrhoea:** *verbal diarrhoea*.

When we combine this affliction with a good helping of witter words and a tendency to tangle our syntax, the result is total obfuscation, or **gobbledegook.**

The former US President George Bush was an acknowledged master of gobbledegook.

- Don't misunderestimate me.
- Chatting with one of the astronauts on the space shuttle *Atlantis:* 'How was the actual deployment thing?' he asks.
- And again, this time in full flow when asked if he would look for ideas on improving education during a forthcoming trip abroad:

Well, I'm going to kick that one right into the end zone of the Secretary of Education. But, yes, we have all—he travels a good deal, goes abroad. We have a lot of people in the department that does that. We're having an international—this is not as much education as dealing with the environment—a big international conference coming up. And we get it all the time, exchanges of ideas. But I think we've got—we set out there and I want to give credit to your Governor McWherter and to your former governor, Lamar Alexander—we've gotten great ideas for a national goals programme from—in this country—from the governors who were responding to, maybe, the principal of your high school, for heaven's sake.

Next time you are tempted to lapse into what reads or sounds like gobbledegook, remember that Texas turkey.

IV. The Jargonaut's Lexicon

Truman decree: 'If you can't convince 'em, confuse 'em'.

Here's a list of jargon words and phrases

> *NOTE:*
> * graded with [J] symbols;
> * the more elusive and impenetrable the jargon, the more [JJJs] it earns.

Learn to recognise jargon, and avoid it if you can.

accentuate [j] stress
accessible [j] As in We intend making Shakespeare accessible to the millions. Use understandable, attractive
accommodation [j] Use home, where you live
accomplish [j] As in accomplish the task. Use complete, finish, do
accordingly [j] Use so
accountability [j] Use responsibility
acquiesce [j] Use agree
acquire [j] Use get, buy, win
activist [j] As in Liberal Party activist. Use worker, campaigner
address [j] As in we must address the problem. Use face, tackle, deal with
adequate [j] Use enough
axiomatic [j] Use obvious
belated [j] Use late

blueprint [jj] As in the proposal is a blueprint for disaster. Use this will end in, means/could mean disaster
chair/chairperson [jj] Use chairman, chairwoman
challenged [jj] As in physically challenged. One of a growing range of euphemisms for personal problems and disabilities. Even in these politically-correct times it is more acceptable to be frank but sensitive. Also avoid differently abled.
come on stream [ii] As in the new model will come on stream in April. Oil producer's jargon usually misapplied. Use begin production, start working, get under way.
come to terms with [ii] Use accept, understand
concept [j] Use idea, plan, proposal, notion
core [jjj] As in core curriculum, core concepts. Use basic
creative accounting [jj] Not necessarily illegal but a vague and troubling term best avoided or left to the financial professionals.
cutback [j] A needless expansion of cut
de-manning [jjj] Use cutting jobs
de-stocking [jj] Use running down stocks, shrinking
downsizing [jjj] Usually meant to mean cutting jobs, or reacting to a bad financial year by cutting back production or services.
downplay [jj] As in he tried to downplay the gravity of the case. Use play down, minimise.
end of the day [j] As in at the end of the day, what have we got? Use in the end
final analysis [j] As in in the final analysis it makes little difference. Use in the end
front-runner [j] Use leading contender, leading or favoured candidate
funded [j] Use paid for

geared [jj] As in *the service was geared to the stockbroker belt*. Use aimed at, intended for, connected to, suited to

generate [j] Use make, produce

hands-on [jj] As in *he adopted a hands-on policy with the staff* It makes you wonder what he was paid to do—massage them? Has been replaced by another jargon word, anyway—proactive.

heading up [jj] As in *Smith will be heading up the takeover team*. Use heading or leading

hidden agenda [jjj] Top-rank jargon. Use hidden/disguised purpose

identify with [jj] As in *He was identified with the activists*. Use associated with, linked with.

implement [jj] Use carry out, fulfil.

inaugurate [jj] As in *She will inaugurate the new policy*. Use introduce, start.

in-flight/in-house [j] Part of the language now but still jargon. When carried further, as in in-car entertainment, it can sound faintly ridiculous.

input [jjjj] As in 'A core post is available for a Senior Research Associate to take a leading role in the programme. The first projects involve relating nursing inputs to patient outcomes in acute hospitals' (University of Newcastle upon Tyne ad). A verbal germ picked up from the computer world where it is used as a verb meaning enter or insert, as in *he inputted the entire file*. Outside computing the word can mean contribute or, as a noun, contribution, or... nothing at all. Avoid.

interface [jjjj] Another refugee from computing. As a noun, it means contact. As a verb, interface with can mean work with, negotiate with, cooperate with or simply meet. Any of these is preferable.

jury is still out [jj] As in Whether the move has saved the pound, the jury is still out. Use is not yet known/decided/certain/clear

meet with, meet up with [jj] Use meet

methodology [j] Often used in error for method. It really means a system of methods and principles

name of the game [jj] As in the name of the game is to make money. Use object

new high, new low [j] Use new/record high level; new/record low level

non-stopping [jjj] As in the eastbound service will be non-stopping at the following stations . . . Use will not stop

operational [j] As in the service is now operational. Use now running/now working

outgoing [j] Use friendly

overview [j] Use broad view

on the back of [jjj] As in the shares rose sharply on the back of the board's profit forecast. Use after/because of/as the result of

ongoing [jjj] As in We have an ongoing supply problem. Use con tinuing/continual/persistent/constant.

precondition [jjj] A condition is something that has to happen before something else will happen. A pre-condition is therefore nonsense, unless you wish to impose a condition on a condition! There must be no preconditions for the peace talks is questionable usage. Best to avoid and use condition.

put on the back burner [jj] Colourful, but jargon nevertheless. Use the more precise postponed/delayed/deferred/suspended, etc.

scenario [jj] As in worst case scenario. Originally meaning an outline of a play or film, its usage has been extended to mean outcome or prediction. Use the more specific words, or result/plan/outline, depending on context.

spend [jj] As in *their total advertising spend will exceed £7m.* A sloppy shortening of expenditure or spending.

state of the art [jj] Use latest/newest.

take on board UI] Use understand/comprehend/accept

terminal [j] Use fatal/mortal

track record [I] Except for an athlete, perhaps, track record means nothing more than record. The next time you are tempted to use proven track record, be a brave pioneer and write experience

user-friendly [jj] Use easy to use

venue[j] Use place/setting

viable alternative [j] Use alternative/choice/option

whitewash [j] As in *They'll certainly want to whitewash the incident.* Use hide, gloss over, cover up, suppress, conceal

V. Cliches to Avoid

accidentally on purpose
accident waiting to happen
actions speak louder than words
act of contrition
acid test
add insult to injury
after due consideration
all intents and purposes
all in the same boat
all over bar the shouting
all things considered
almost too good to be true
angel of mercy
angry silence (classic Darby and Joan)
as a matter of fact
as luck would have it
as sure as eggs is/are eggs
at the end of the day
at this moment/point in time
auspicious occasion
avid reader
baby with the bathwater, don't throw out the
backseat driver
back to basics/to the drawing board
bag and baggage
bag of tricks
ballpark figure
ball's in your court, the
bang your head against a brick wall
barking up the wrong tree

bat an eyelid (try wink and surprise everyone)
batten down the hatches
beavering away
beer and skittles, it's not all
before you can say Jack Robinson
beggars can't be choosers
be good (and if you can't be good, be careful!)
be that as it may
between a rock and a hard place
bite the bullet
blessing in disguise
blind leading the blind
blissful ignorance
blood out of a stone, it's like trying to get
bloody but unbowed
blow hot and cold
blot on the landscape
blow the whistle
blue rinse brigade
blushing bride
bone of contention
borrowed time
bottom line
breath of fresh air
bright eyed and bushy tailed
brought to book
brownie points
bruising battle/encounter
bumper to bumper traffic jam
by the same token
call it a day
callow youth
calm before the storm
camp as a row of tents
can of worms
captive audience

card up his sleeve
cards stacked against us
cardinal sin
carte blanche
cast of thousands
Catch 22 situation
catalogue of errors/misery/disaster/misfortune
cat among the pigeons, put the
catholic tastes
caustic comment
cautious optimism
centre of the universe
chalk and cheese, as different as
champing at the bit
chapter and verse
chapter of accidents
cheek by jowl
cheque's in the post, the
cheap and cheerful
cherished belief
chew the cud/fat
chop and change
chorus of approval/dispproval
chosen few
circumstances beyond our
control cold light of day, in the
cold water on, pour
come home to roost
comes to the crunch, when it
common or garden
compulsive viewing/reading
conspicious by his/her absence
cool as a cucumber
cool, calm and collected
copious notes (and, if made by a reporter, usually scribbled notes)

crack of dawn
crazy like a fox
creme de la creme
crisis of confidence
cross that bridge when we come to it we'll
cry over spilt milk
current climate, in the
cut a long story short, to
cut and dried
cut any ice, it doesn't/won't
cutting edge
damn with faint praise
Darby and Joan
darkest hour is just before dawn dark secret
day in, day out
dead as a dodo
dead in the water
deadly accurate
dead of night, in the
dead to the world
deafening silence
deaf to entreaties
death's door, at
death warmed up, like
depths of depravity
desert a sinking ship
despite misgivings
devour every word (and then there are none left to hang on to)
dicing with death
dim and distant past, in the
dog eat dog
donkey's years ago, it was
don't call us, we'll call you
don't count your chickens before they're hatched

doom and gloom merchants
dot the i's and cross the t's
drop of a hat, at the
dry as a bone
dyed in the wool
each and everyone
eager beaver
eagerly devour
ear to the ground
easier said than done
eat humble pie
eat your heart out
economical with the truth
empty nest, empty nesters, empty nest syndrome
enfant terrible
eternal regret/ eternal shame, to my
every dog has his day
every man jack of them
everything but the kitchen sink
every little helps
every stage of the game, at
explore every avenue
face the facts/music
fact of the matter, the
fair and square
fair sex, the
fall between two stools/by the wayside
fall on deaf ears
far and wide
far be it from me
fast and furious
fast lane, in the
fate worse than death
feel-good factor, the
few and far between
field day, having a

fighting fit final insult
fine-tooth comb, go/went through it with a
finger in every pie
finger of suspicion
firing on all cylinders
first and foremost
first things
first fish out of water
fit as a fiddle
fits and starts, in/by
flash in the pan
flat as a pancake
flat denial flavour of the month
flog a dead horse
fly in the ointment fond belief
food for thought
footloose and fancy free
forlorn hope
fraught with danger/peril
free, gratis and for nothing
frenzy of activity
from the sublime to the ridiculous
from the word go
fudge the issue
fullness of time, in the
funny ha-ha or funny peculiar?
F-word
gainful employment
gameplan
generous to a fault
gentle giant
gentleman's agreement
gentler sex, the
girl Friday
give a dog a bad name
give him an inch and he'll take a yard

give up the ghost
glowing tribute
glutton for punishment
goes without saying, it
goes from strength to strength
golden opportunity good as gold
go off half-cocked
gory details, the
grasp the nettle
greatest thing since sliced bread
great unwashed, the
green with envy
grim death, like
grin and bear it
grind/ground to a halt
grist to the mill
guardian angel
hale and hearty
hand in glove with
handle with kid gloves
hand over fist
hand to mouth existence
handwriting is on the wall
hanged for a sheep as a lamb, we might as well be
happy accident/event/hunting ground/medium
happily ensconced
hard and fast rule
has what it takes
having said that
have a nice one
have got a lot on my plate, I've
have I got news for you?
head and shoulders above
heaping ridicule
heart and soul
heart's in the right place, his/her

hell or high water
high and dry
hit or miss
hit the nail on the head
hit the panic button
hive of activity
Hobson's choice
hold your horses
hoist with his own petard
honest truth, the
hope against hope
horns of a dilemma, on the
horses for courses
howling gale
how long is a piece of string?
how time flies
If the worst comes to the worst
if you can't beat 'em, join 'em
if you can't stand the heat get out of the kitchen
if you've got it, flaunt it
ignorance is bliss
ill-gotten gains
ill-starred venture
impossible dream, an/the
in all conscience/honesty
in a nutshell
inch-by-inch search
in less than no time
in one ear and out the other
inordinate amount of
in the pipeline
in this day and age
iota, not one
it never rains but it pours
it's a small world
it's not the end of the world
it stands to reason
it will all come out in the wash
it will all end in tears

it will soon blow over
ivory tower
jack of all trades (but master of none)
jaundiced eye
jewel in the crown
Johnny-come-lately
jockey for position
jump on the bandwagon
jump the gun
just deserts
just for the record
just what the doctor ordered
keep a low profile
keep a straight face
keep my/your head above water
keep the wolf from the door
keep your chin up
keep your nose clean
keep your nose to the grindstone
kickstart
kill two birds with one stone
kill with kindness kiss of death
knee-high to a grasshopper
knocked into a cocked hat
knocked/knocks the spots off
know the ropes
know which side your bread's buttered on
knuckle under
labour of love
lack-lustre performance
lap of luxury
large as lift/larger than life
last but not least
last straw, it's the
late in the day
laugh all the way to the bank

laugh up your sleeve
lavish praise/hospitality/ceremony
lay it on with a trowel
leading light
leave/left in the lurch
leave no stone unturned '(or as the bird hater said, leave no tern unstoned)
let bygones be bygones
let's get this show on the road
let sleeping dogs lie
let well alone
lick his/their wounds
level playing field
light at the end of the tunnel
like a house on fire
little the wiser
little woman
live and let live
local difficulty, a little
lock, stock and barrel
long arm of the law
long hot summer
long time no see loose end, at a
lost cause
lost in admiration
lost in contemplation
love you and leave you, I must
made of sterner stuff
made/make a killing
make a mountain out of a molehill
make an offer I can't refuse
make ends meet
make hay while the sun shines
make no bones about it
make my day
make or break make/making short work of it

make/making the best of a bad job
make/making tracks
man after my own heart, a
make/making waves
manna from heaven
man of straw/man of the world
man to man
many hands
make light work
mark my words
matter of life and death
method in his madness
Midas touch, the
millstone around your neck
mind boggles, the
mixed blessing (and a variation, it was not an unmixed blessing...)
model of its kind/propriety
moment of truth
moot point
more haste, less speed
more in sorrow than in anger
more than meets the eye
more the merrier, the
mortgaged to the hilt
movers and shakers
move the goalposts
much-needed reforms
much of a muchness
muddy the waters
mutton dressed as lamb
nail in his coffin, put/drive a
name of the game, the
nearest and dearest
necessity is the mother of invention
neck and neck

needle in a haystack
needless to say
neither here nor there
new lease of life
nick of time, in the
nine-day/day's wonder
nip it in the bud/nipped in the bud
nitty-gritty
no expense spared
no names, no pack drill
no news is good news
no peace for the wicked
no problem
no skin off my nose
no spring chicken
nothing to write home about
nothing ventured, nothing gained
not just a pretty face
not out of the woods yet
not to be sneezed at
not to put too fine a point on it
now or never
odd man out
odds and ends
off the beaten track
off the cuff
old as the hills
older and wiser
once bitten, twice shy
once in a blue moon
one fell swoop
one in a million
only time will tell
on the ball
on the level
on the spur of the moment

on the tip of my tongue
out of sight,
out of mind
out of the blue
out on a limb
over and done with
over my dead body
over the top
own goal, score an
own worst enemy
packed in like sardines
painstaking investigation
pale into insignificance
palpable nonsense
paper over the cracks
par for the course
part and parcel
pass muster
past its/his/her sell-by date
patter of tiny feet
pay through your nose
pecking order
picture of health
piece de resistance
pie in the sky
pinpoint accuracy
plain as a pikestaff
plain as the nose on your face
play your cards right
pleased as Punch
point of no return
poisoned chalice
pound of flesh
powers that be, the
practice makes perfect
press on regardless

pride and joy
pride of place
proof of the pudding
pull out all the stops
pure as the driven snow
put on hold/the back burner
put two and two together
put up or shut up
put your best foot forward
put your foot down
put your money where your mouth is
put your nose out of joint
quality of life
quantum leap
queer the pitch
quick and the dead
quid pro quo
quiet before the storm, the
race against time
rack and ruin, going to
raining cats and dogs (and hailing taxis)
rat race, the
read my lips
red rag to a bull, like a
reinventing the wheel
reliable source (the reporter's friend)
resounding silence
right as rain
rings a bell
rings true
risk life and limb
rock the boat, don't
Rome wasn't built in a day
rose by any other name, a
rotten apple in a barrel, one
rough diamond, a

ruffledfrathers
ruled with a rod of iron
run it up the flagpole (and see who salutes)
run of the mill
run to seed
safe and sound
sailing close to the wind
sale of the century
salt of the earth
saved by the bell
search high and low
second to none
seething cauldron
see eye to eye
see how the land lies
see the wood for the trees, can't
sell like hot cakes
serial gossiper/meddler/bullshit artist etc
serious money
set in stone/concrete
shape or form, in any
share and share alike
ships that pass in the night
shoot yourself in the foot!
shot himself in the foot
short and sweet
shot across the bows
sick and tired
sick as a parrot
sight for sore eyes
signed, sealed and delivered
silent majority the
simmering hatred
sitting duck
sixes and sevens
six of one and half-a-dozen of the other

skating on thin ice
skin of his teeth
slaving over a hot stove all day, I've been
slowly but surely
smell a rat
snatch defeat from the jaws of victory (and, of course, vice versa!)
so far so good
solid as a rock
so near and yet so far
sorely needed
sour grapes
splendid isolation
square peg in a round hole
straight and narrow, stick to the
straight from the shoulder
strange as it may seem!
strange to relate
strike while the iron's hot
suffer fools gladly, he/she doesn't
suffer in silence survival of the fittest
sugar the pill
sweetness and light, all
swept off his fret
swings and roundabouts
tail between his legs, he went off with his
take it with a grain of salt
take the bull by the horns
take the rough with the smooth
tarred with the same brush
teach your mother/grandmother to suck eggs
technological wizardry
teething troubles
tender loving care (TLC)
tender mercies
terra firma

thankful for small mercies, be
that's life
that's the way the cookie crumbles
there but for the grace of God go I
thereby hangs a tale
there's no such thing as a free lunch
this day and age
throw in the towel
thunderous applause
tighten your belts
time flies
time heals everything
time waits for no man
tip of the iceberg
tissue of lies
to all intents and purposes
tomorrow is another day
too little, too late
to my dying day too awful
terrible/horrible to contemplate
too many cooks (spoil the broth)
too numerous to mention
torrential rain
towering inferno
tower of strength
trials and tribulations
turn a deaf ear
turn over a new leaf
twenty-twenty hindsight
twinkling of an eye
in a twisted him around
her little finger
two's company, three's a crowd
ultra-sophisticated
unacceptable face of capitalism (or any other institution you
   want to knock)

unavoidable delay
unalloyed delight
unconscionable time, taking an/unconscionable liar
under a cloud
under the weather
unequal task
university of life
unkindest cut of all
unsung heroes
untimely end
untold wealth
unvarnished truth
up to scratch/not up to scratch
upper crust
vanish into thin air
variety is the spice of life
vested interest vicious circle
vote with their feet
wages of sin (is death)
waited on hand and foot
walking on air/eggs
walking on broken glass
waste not, want not
water under the bridge
wealth of experience/material/knowledge
wedded bliss
weighed in the balance and found wanting
well-earned rest
wheels within wheels
when the cat's away the mice will play
when the going gets tough (the tough get going)
whiter than white
winter of discontent
with all due respect
with bated breath
with malice aforethought

without a shadow of a doubt
without fear of contradiction
woman scorned, hell hath no fury like a
wonders will never cease
word to the Wise, a
work my fingers to the bone,
world's your oyster,
the writing's on the wall, the
wrong end of the stick, you've got the
yawning gulf
year in, year out
you can bet your bottom dollar/last penny
you can lead a horse to water but you can't make him drink
you can't make a silk purse out of a sow's ear
you can't teach an old dog new tricks
you can't win 'em all
you could have knocked me down with a feather
you get what you pay for
you pays your money and takes your choice
your guess is as good as mine
you're breaking my heart
you're only young once

Avoid being a cliché-holic

Power-check

- Take some time to think out what you want to say before you begin to write
- While you are writing, test your prose phrase by phrase, sentence by sentence, to make sure you are expressing exactly what you want to say
- When you have finished, re-read every sentence carefully and ensure that nothing can be misunderstood.

VI. The Fog Index

1. Choose a section of the written work, at least 100 words long. Count the exact number of words.
2. Count the number of sentences. If a long sentence contains two or more complete thoughts, separated by commas, colons or semi-colons, treat each thought as a sentence.
3. Divide the total number of words by the total number of sentences. That will give you the average sentence length.
4. Now go through the same passage, counting the number of words of three or more syllables. Ignore proper names, words that are combinations of short, easy words (such as caretaker, bookkeeper, headmaster) and words which are of three syllables because an -ed, -s, or -es has been added to the basic word (like invented, transpose-s).
5. Now (getting out your calculator would be wise at this point) find the percentage of multi-syllable words by dividing the multi-syllable total by the overall word total, and multiplying the result by 100.
6. Add this figure to your average sentence-length figure, and multiply the total by 0.4 (you can now see the reason for the calculator!)

Here's an example of the procedure:

1. Length of passage (word count) = 110
2. Number of sentences = 7
3. Average sentence length (110 divided by 7) = 16
4. Number of words of 3 + syllables = 12
5. Percentage of multi-syllable words
   (12 divided by 110 multiplied by 100) = 11
6. Fog Index (11 + 16 = 27 multiplied by 0.4) = 10.8

An Index of 10.8 would qualify as about average: clear, understandable, but capable of improvement.

Now let us apply the Fog Index to some examples of published writing.

A fortnight today India's future in the global economy will be decided. / Not by the voters of India, / but by the voters of the world: / Our Government has made it clear that if the world says 'Non' in their referendum, the development is stalled. / If they say 'YES', we can all go happily forward with no regard to how the Indian people may feel. / This is unacceptable. / Our people have never had the chance to vote on European economy / Global economy was not an Election issue / so it is quite arguable that India should have a referendum. / the financial gurus believe that this kind of poll is 'undemocratic'. / Surely it can't be wrong if the ordinary man and woman—as well as MPs—have their say /

Total words:	122
Over two syllables:	11
Percentage:	9
Total sentences:	12
Average sentence length:	10
Add:	10 + 9 = 19
Multiply by:	0.4
Fog Index:	7.6 = sparklingly clear

Style Colour
(Elements of Style)

Writing elegant, expressive prose

One of the greatest stylists in English, Somerset Maugham, put it this way: 'A good style should show no sign of effort. What is written should seem a happy accident'.

Writing is the paint job, to cover all the construction.

We throw the verbs and nouns in the air and juggle the adverbs and adjectives to produce some inspirational prose, and perhaps we're not quite there yet.

While the mind dictates what is to be written, the ear monitors what is going down on paper—or at least it should. Writers with a tin ear are never likely to write with precision, brevity and elegance—or with style. And so we have the great epic (blind) poet MILTON.

Just as certain blends of musical notes stir us deeply in some mysterious way, so certain combinations of words possess the strange power to freeze us in our tracks, to inspire us, to echo in our minds for a lifetime.

The box of grammatical tricks is not enough for the magic.

One ought to try and transcend the box of tricks and create real magical prose: learn to write good, crisp, clear English, which is no mean accomplishment.

Style is the way in which writers use the language to express themselves.

The magic wand:
- Polishing
- Burnishing

- ☞ Simplifying
- ☞ Colouring our writing
- ☞ Developing a critical ear
- ☞ Learning from writers who please and thrill us
- ☞ Practicing our box of tricks.

The Basics

Achieving good writing is a learning process.

And like all learning, start with the simple: simple, clear prose—no pyrotechnics, no words or expressions you don't quite understand—just tell it like it is.

Remember Dr Samuel Johnson's advice:

'Read over your compositions, and wherever you meet with a passage which you think is particularly fine, strike it out'.

Communicate with the Reader

Plain writing need not be dull writing. On the contrary, a good writer always keeps the reader foremost in mind, thinking constantly.

If the warning bell rings a good writer unhesitatingly changes a word, switches a phrase around, rewrites and reviews again. . . and again. Sounds like hard work. But the end product is worth it and can be very satisfying.

Word gym

Go down to the **'word gym'** and practise some exercises. Writing directions will get rid of the flab.

Important

Every good writer needs some humility!

Brevity

Build on Brevity

Vigorous writing is concise:
- ☞ A sentence should contain no unnecessary words
- ☞ A paragraph should contain no unnecessary sentences, for the same reason that a drawing should have no unnecessary lines and a machine no unnecessary parts.
- ☞ Every word must tell.

Brevity does not mean the extreme terseness of telegram-speak.

Few people these days want to write more words than necessary, or to be forced to read two hundred words when the information could have been conveyed in a hundred.

Earlier we saw how, by combining simple sentences into compound sentences, we can economise on words and even enhance clarity; but there is another grammatical convention that allows us to trim away words we don't need, or 'sentence fat'. It's called **ellipsis,** and it works like this:

Without Ellipsis

✗ When the children were called to the dinner table they came to the dinner table immediately

With Ellipsis

✓ When the children were called to the dinner table they came immediately.

Alexander Pope's advice on brevity is as sound today as it was nearly three centuries ago:
Words are like leaves; and where they most abound,
Much *fruit of sense* beneath is very rarely found.
Or, to *further encapsulate* the thought: lean is keen.

Change Gear: Active To Passive

ACTIVE   Her boyfriend bought the gift.
PASSIVE   The ring was bought by her boyfriend.

It's easy to see why one kind of sentence is called active and the other passive; active sentences are direct and personal and seem more interesting, while passive sentences tend to be detached and impersonal by comparison.

> *NOTE:* If you are writing a scientific or academic article, then passive would be appropriate; otherwise use the active voice:

My father painted those pictures which were left to me.
☞ That sentence begins with the active voice (My father painted those pictures) but then switches to the passive (which were left to me). What the sentence should have said is, *My father painted those pictures and left them to me.* Follow the logic: my father did both things—painted the pictures and (presumably) left them to me.

Mixing active and passive expressions isn't the only source of discord in a sentence. Discord comes when a singular noun takes a singular verb and a plural noun takes a plural verb:

✗ We was furious with the officer's decision.
   The four cars isn't for sale.

✓ We were furious with the officer's decision.
   The four cars aren't for sale.

In longer sentences watch out:
   The Committee has just a week (to January 17) to announce their initial findings.
   Clearly either has/its or have/their are required.

Shifting from personal to impersonal pronouns in the same sentence (and vice versa) is another common mistake:
- ✗ If one is to keep out of trouble, you should mind your own business.

NOTE: Either stay with one or the personal (preferred) you.

The **positive** will vastly improve your writing style:
That dog is not unlike the one I saw in town yesterday.
That dog is similar to the one I saw in town yesterday.

Colour Your Word Palette

Figures of Speech

You may be writing in monochrome: without the vibrancy, the variety, the sensuality and fun of colour!

Then what you need is a **paintbox of verbal effects,** a word palette of literary devices called figures of speech: metaphor, simile, hyperbole, alliteration and wordplay.

Metaphor

We're surrounded by everyday metaphors: *raining cats and dogs, mouth of the river, stony silence, he sailed into him, over the moon* . . . thousands of them are irrevocably part of the language. The difficulty is in inventing new ones, and writers who can, and can inject them at appropriate places in their texts, are a step ahead of the rest of us.

The beauty of metaphor is that it has the ability to bring a dull expression vividly to life, and explain a difficult concept with startling clarity.

Metaphor is describing something by using an analogy

with something quite different. If we hear that a person '*has egg on his face*' we are expected to know that he wasn't the victim of an egg-thrower, but has been left in a very embarrassing situation. Egg and embarrassment are connected only by a wild flight of imagination (metaphor and cliché!).

Invent new metaphors but try to avoid creaky old ones. And in particular, watch out for mixed metaphors such as:

✗ They were treading in uncharted waters and I smell a rat but I'll nip him in the bud.

Simile

A simile makes a direct comparison between two dissimilar things:

- as fit as a fiddle
- as good as gold
- as sick as a parrot
- he's crazy (like a fox, ears like jug handles.)

> *NOTE:* Invariably similes are introduced by the conjunction **as** or the preposition **like**.

A simile can enliven a piece of writing, but it should preferably be original; as with metaphors, creating apt similes is a special art.

Fun With Similes:

- Robert Burns (My love is like a red, red rose)
- Wordsworth (I wandered lonely as a cloud)
- Cecil Day Lewis (A girl who stands like a questioning iris by the waterside)

Tired simile-avoidance techniques are needed to prevent our writing being clogged by such simles:

- Sharp as a razor
- Dull as ditchwater
- Pleased as Punch
- Mad as a March hare.

Hyperbole

Hyperbole is deliberate overstatement: wild exaggeration used to make an emphatic point.

- I'm dying of hunger: I could eat a horse

Hyperbole has to be witty or outrageous to succeed.

Hyperbolic Classics

- I got legless last night
- He couldn't fight his way out of a paper bag;
- A diamond that would choke a horse.

Alliteration and Wordplay

Use this sparingly.

Some pastel shades: word palette.

Alliteration

- Sing a song of Sixpence
- Peter Piper picked a peck of pickled peppers

The repetition of stressed sounds in words adjacent or near one another.

- *To sit in solemn silence in a dull, dark dock / In a pestilential prison, with a life-long lock / Awaiting the sensation of a short, sharp shock / From a cheap and chippy chopper on a big, black block!*

Colloquialism And Idiom

Knowing when and where to use colloquial, idiomatic and slang expressions is a matter of style and experience:
- Get cracking
- Give us a break
- Part and parcel
- Keep a straight face
- Pass the buck
- Odds and ends (idioms)
- *bimbo, ankle biter, sprog, muttonhead, jollies, tosser* (slang).

Litotes

Litotes is understatement, the opposite of hyperbole
- This is no easy task
- He was not a little upset
- Not uncommon
- Not a bad teacher.

Litotes is a way of asserting a statement by denying its opposite: *not bad* means good, fine, okay.

NOTE: Litotes can convey fine shades of meaning, so use this device carefully.

Synecdoche

This is a figurative device in which a part is substituted for the whole, or the whole for a part.
- We sent twenty heads to Pakistan today. (i.e. We sent twenty cattle. The expression uses part of the cow to indicate the whole).

☞ India beat Australia by three wickets. (Here the whole—India and Australia—is used to indicate a part—the Indian and Australian cricket teams).

> *NOTE:* The device is useful in achieving brevity and avoiding repetition. One of the most common synecdochic expressions is **man**, which, in the sense of mankind, is only part of a whole, man and woman.

Bungee Jumping

Don't come down with a crash!

Writing is like bungee jumping! Perhaps learning to write fluently is a bit like learning to fly. Once you experience the heady feeling of being airborne and solo, the sky's the limit. Learn to temper your newfound skills with caution.

☞ Brevity is beautiful. So is simplicity. Short words too. And short sentences.
☞ Prefer concrete to abstract words
☞ Prefer the active voice to the passive
☞ Prefer positive expressions to negative
☞ Keep sentences harmonious—in voice, tense and number
☞ Listen to your sentences
☞ Attract and keep the reader's attention
☞ Think precision
☞ Think poetry

The Bottomline

Be Yourself; 'When I write, I write so much like me'.

Remember the poem of Ogden Nash

So That's Who I Remind Me Of

When I consider men of golden talents,
I'm delighted, in my introverted way,
To discover, as I'm drawing up the balance,
How much we have in common, I and they.

Like Burns, I have a weakness for the bottle,
Like Shakespeare, little Latin and less Greek;
I bite my fingernails like Aristotle;
Like Thackeray, I have a snobbish streak.

I'm afflicted with the vanity of Byron,
I've inherited the spitefulness of Pope;
Like Petrarch, I'm a sucker for a siren,
Like Milton, I've a tendency to mope.

My spelling is suggestive of a Chaucer;
Like Johnson, well, I do not wish to die
(I also drink my coffee from the saucer);
And if Goldsmith was a parrot, so am I.

. . . .

In comparison with men of golden talents,
I am all a man of talent ought to be;
I resemble every genius in his vice, however heinous—
Yet I write so much like me.